Lumion 3D Best Practices

Explore the best practices to build architectural
visualizations efficiently in Lumion 3D

Ciro Cardoso

PUBLISHING

BIRMINGHAM - MUMBAI

Lumion 3D Best Practices

First published: June 2015

Production Reference: 1250615

Published by Packt Publishing Ltd.
Livery Place
35 Livery Street
Birmingham B3 2PB, UK.

ISBN 978-1-78355-085-2

www.packtpub.com

Credits

Author
Ciro Cardoso

Reviewers
CJ Arquitecto
Peter-Daniel Fazakas
Filip Joveski
Gianfranco Maiorano

Commissioning Editor
Kunal Parikh

Acquisition Editor
Subho Gupta

Content Development Editor
Prachi Bisht

Technical Editor
Vivek Pala

Copy Editors
Brandt DMello
Neha Vyas

Project Coordinator
Shipra Chawhan

Proofreader
Safis Editing

Indexer
Mariammal Chettiyar

Graphics
Disha Haria

Production Coordinator
Nilesh R. Mohite

Cover Work
Nilesh R. Mohite

About the Author

Ciro Cardoso is an experienced 3D artist and a trained author with an architectural background who started experimenting with creative software and 3D software back in 2000.

In 2005, he was running his own small multimedia business and worked on projects as diverse as graphic designing, CAD services, and architectural visualization; more recently, he started using Lumion successfully for high-end projects in more than six countries. He is quite literate with software in general, with extensive expertise with Maya, 3ds Max, AutoCAD, Photoshop, Lumion, Unreal 4, and Bentley MicroStation.

He is also the author of several books about Lumion and is now working in London.

About the Reviewers

CJ Arquitecto is a young Portuguese architect born in Lagos, Portugal, in June, 1984.

At the age of 24, he completed his degree in architecture at the University of Porto, also known as the Faculty of Architecture of the University of Porto, designed by the architect Siza Vieira. In 2011, he started using Lumion while he worked on urbanism projects in 3D works designed for Angolan customers. He has participated in several national and international architectural contests and has won two awards. Also, he has been developing several architectural projects, mostly in Angola; these include projects that range from residential houses to sports complex centers. His works can be searched on the Behance or Archinect websites (`archinect.com/cjarchitect`). In 2015, he started his own photography business and did event photography in Portugal. You can visit his works and more information on `cjphoto2015.wordpress.com`. Also, he reviewed books on Lumion 3D in 2013 and 2014, which has led him to contribute to the reviewing process of this book.

Peter-Daniel Fazakas is an architect and designer born in Bucharest, Romania. Growing up in a family of intellectuals, scientists, and artists, Peter was fascinated by hand drawing and CAD software from his early childhood. He decided to study architecture at "Ion Mincu" University of Architecture and Urbanism in Bucharest, where he later graduated with an MArch degree.

Working as an architect and art director in Romania, France, Cyprus, and China, he has gained experience in architecture, graphic design, 3D rendering, 3D animation, and augmented reality. These have played a big role in his fascination for experimenting with new computer software.

Currently living in Shanghai, he is involved in large-scale architectural projects. A couple of years ago, Peter started his small Bucharest-based architecture and design company, and he is always available to quickly respond to prospective clients. He likes sports, music, and cooking.

Filip Joveski is a licensed architect and 3D artist. He was first introduced to the 3D world in 2002 in a 3D modeling class at the university that he attended. After getting his degree in architecture, he worked at several different firms in different countries for a great deal of demanding clients.

He is currently employed at an architectural office in Germany, where he works as the head of the visualization team. There, he creates images, animations, illustrations, and has many projects behind him. He designed various types of objects and spaces, including houses, apartments, lofts, restaurants, and unique interior designs, ranging from sketches of the floor plans, sections, 3D modeling, and other renderings. He also worked on *Mastering Lumion 3D*, *Packt Publishing*, as a reviewer.

He is proficient in software in general and has extensive expertise in 3ds Max, ArchiCAD, Maya, AutoCAD, SketchUp, Photoshop, Lumion, and Artlantis. He also expresses his creative streak through many of his paintings and sculptures. He has extraordinary hand drafting skills. His sense of color, texture, and depth has greatly helped him in the world of 3D modeling and visualization.

Gianfranco Maiorano is a creative and talented architect and an EU-licensed construction engineer based in London, UK, since 2013. He studied and completed his master's degree in architecture and construction engineering from the University of Bologna, Italy. He has experience in both public and private projects in the UK and Italy, including several competition submissions.

He is the founder and director of gfm Studio Lab. Established in August 2014 and based in London, gfm Studio Lab provides services from architecture to design and provides art for architectural firms and private clients that particularly work in the retail and residential sector.

Since childhood, he has been very passionate about architecture. Possessing a natural intellectual capacity and curiosity about his chosen field, he is driven by a keen interest in researching contemporary architecture, art, and digital tools, especially in connection with quantum physics and parametric and generative techniques for architecture.

He has exceptional technical expertise with regard to a wide range of software from 3D modeling and BIM to visualization and animation.

He finds inspiration from artists such as Lucio Fontana, Antony Gormley, and Anish Kapoor and architects such as Renzo Piano, Ben van Berkel, and Rem Koolhaas.

You can contact him through his website at www.gianfrancomaiorano.com.

www.PacktPub.com

Support files, eBooks, discount offers, and more

For support files and downloads related to your book, please visit www.PacktPub.com.

Did you know that Packt offers eBook versions of every book published, with PDF and ePub files available? You can upgrade to the eBook version at www.PacktPub.com and as a print book customer, you are entitled to a discount on the eBook copy. Get in touch with us at service@packtpub.com for more details.

At www.PacktPub.com, you can also read a collection of free technical articles, sign up for a range of free newsletters and receive exclusive discounts and offers on Packt books and eBooks.

https://www2.packtpub.com/books/subscription/packtlib

Do you need instant solutions to your IT questions? PacktLib is Packt's online digital book library. Here, you can search, access, and read Packt's entire library of books.

Why subscribe?

- Fully searchable across every book published by Packt
- Copy and paste, print, and bookmark content
- On demand and accessible via a web browser

Free access for Packt account holders

If you have an account with Packt at www.PacktPub.com, you can use this to access PacktLib today and view 9 entirely free books. Simply use your login credentials for immediate access.

Table of Contents

Preface

Lumion has a strong presence in the visualization field as a useful, practical, and efficient tool to create beautiful architectural visualizations in a quick and efficient way.

The need to write this book started with the necessity to find proficient ways to work with Lumion and to simplify its workflow. If you think about it, there are several stages that we need to go through before we present a Lumion visualization. Each stage presents its unique challenges, in particular, if you are new to the 3D world. As an example, at the importing stage, you don't simply import a 3D model in Lumion. You have to confirm whether the geometry is optimized and that there aren't any overlapping faces and you also need to check whether each surface has a material that can be used in Lumion.

Yes, Lumion is an intuitive tool, but that doesn't mean it will do all the hard work for you. That is why you have this book, which covers the most important stages of Lumion and helps you understand the ways in which you can take full advantage of Lumion's capabilities.

This book doesn't have any examples for you to follow, for just a simple reason; you want a book that is practical and efficient without wasting time following an example that has nothing to do with your project. Certainly, you may want something that you can apply straight away to your project and see first-hand how things really work. For that reason, I encourage you to read this book while working on your projects and then, later, you can use it as a quick reference.

What this book covers

Chapter 1, Getting Ready with Lumion 3D, focuses primarily on the first steps to be taken with Lumion, and this will help you to understand what is available inside Lumion and how to bridge the gap of the lack of models. Two additional topics are covered in this chapter to help you start a project in Lumion on the right foot: the use of layers and how materials are essential while importing a 3D model.

Chapter 2, Importing and Handling 3D Models, will help you to import 3D models from any application and will show you how to tackle specific problems while importing 3D models. You will also learn how to import 3D models and work with large scenes. After importing, After importing, the next stage will involve how to place and handle a group of 3D models.

Chapter 3, Creating an Interior Scene with Lumion, covers different techniques to create interior scenes with efficiency and interior scenes. This involves three sections: one that covers 3D models and how you can take full advantage of the Context and the Properties menu, the second that helps us with the materials, and the third to create an interior lighting rig.

Chapter 4, Creating an Exterior Scene with Lumion, will help you to handle the different technical aspects that compose a landscape. A more in-depth look will provide you with the best techniques to create different landscape types. A special section in this chapter is aimed at helping you with the sculpting of the terrain and will show you the different techniques available to modify the terrain.

Chapter 5, Working with Physically Based Materials, provides you with all the help you need to start working with the physically based rendering materials (PBR) that are a fundamental aspect to create believable visualizations. You will learn what makes them so special and also three different techniques to create materials in Lumion.

Chapter 6, Animation Techniques in Lumion, explores how to turn a lifeless 3D world into a vibrant world full of animations and life. Some technical and advanced tools are also covered in this chapter to give you full control over Lumion's camera.

Chapter 7, Producing a Still Image with Lumion, is the first part of two chapters that explains how to use Lumion's effects in the **Photo** mode to produce believable visualizations by mimicking what is present in the real world.

Chapter 8, Producing a Movie with Lumion, is the second chapter that gives you additional information about Lumion's effects. This chapter also provides you with information about how to create, organize, and combine small animation clips to create a beautiful movie.

Chapter 9, Exporting and Post Production, has some important information regarding the best ways to optimize your scenes before you export or render them. The two important sections that we've covered here are how to use render passes for an efficient workflow and how to use Lumion Viewer.

What you need for this book

Lumion version 4 is used for all the examples in this book, but you can follow the explanations using the free version or a previous Lumion version. Although Adobe Photoshop is used in some examples, you can use GIMP as an alternative.

Who this book is for

This book is designed for all levels of Lumion users, from beginners to advanced-level users. In this book, you will find useful insights and professional techniques to improve and develop your skills in order to fully control and master Lumion. However, this book doesn't cover the process of transforming 2D information (a CAD plan) into a 3D model.

Conventions

In this book, you will find a number of text styles that distinguish between different kinds of information. Here are some examples of these styles and an explanation of their meaning.

Code words in text, database table names, folder names, filenames, file extensions, pathnames, dummy URLs, user input, and Twitter handles are shown as follows: "Lumion lets you save a stack of effects as a Lumion movie effects file (*1me) that can be loaded into a different project."

New terms and **important words** are shown in bold. Words that you see on the screen, for example, in menus or dialog boxes, appear in the text like this: "When clicking on the **Save Movie** button, the initial option available is the **MP4** tab and the options to export are very simple."

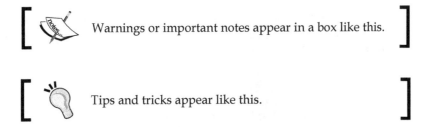

[Warnings or important notes appear in a box like this.]

[Tips and tricks appear like this.]

Reader feedback

Feedback from our readers is always welcome. Let us know what you think about this book—what you liked or disliked. Reader feedback is important for us as it helps us develop titles that you will really get the most out of.

To send us general feedback, simply e-mail feedback@packtpub.com, and mention the book's title in the subject of your message.

If there is a topic that you have expertise in and you are interested in either writing or contributing to a book, see our author guide at www.packtpub.com/authors.

Customer support

Now that you are the proud owner of a Packt book, we have a number of things to help you to get the most from your purchase.

Downloading the color images of this book

We also provide you with a PDF file that has color images of the screenshots/ diagrams used in this book. The color images will help you better understand the changes in the output. You can download this file from `https://www.packtpub.com/ sites/default/files/downloads/0852OT_B01892_Lumion3D_Best_Practices_ ColorImage.pdf`.

Errata

Although we have taken every care to ensure the accuracy of our content, mistakes do happen. If you find a mistake in one of our books—maybe a mistake in the text or the code—we would be grateful if you could report this to us. By doing so, you can save other readers from frustration and help us improve subsequent versions of this book. If you find any errata, please report them by visiting `http://www.packtpub. com/submit-errata`, selecting your book, clicking on the **Errata Submission Form** link, and entering the details of your errata. Once your errata are verified, your submission will be accepted and the errata will be uploaded to our website or added to any list of existing errata under the Errata section of that title.

To view the previously submitted errata, go to `https://www.packtpub.com/books/ content/support` and enter the name of the book in the search field. The required information will appear under the **Errata** section.

Piracy

Piracy of copyrighted material on the Internet is an ongoing problem across all media. At Packt, we take the protection of our copyright and licenses very seriously. If you come across any illegal copies of our works in any form on the Internet, please provide us with the location address or website name immediately so that we can pursue a remedy.

Please contact us at `copyright@packtpub.com` with a link to the suspected pirated material.

We appreciate your help in protecting our authors and our ability to bring you valuable content.

Questions

If you have a problem with any aspect of this book, you can contact us at `questions@packtpub.com`, and we will do our best to address the problem.

1
Getting Ready with Lumion 3D

What was your initial reaction when you discovered Lumion 3D and what you can do with it? Perhaps, it was an absolute astonishment since Lumion 3D is a remarkable software and at the same time, it is easy to use. Personally, I have been using Lumion since its first version and with each new version, Lumion's team doesn't stop surprising me with new tools and the ability to almost effortlessly produce artistic impressions, believable renders, and incredible videos in a very reasonable amount of time.

However, Lumion 3D has some limitations and is not a magical solution that will automatically create beautiful concepts and illustrations. Some will say that it takes only 15 minutes to make a a final product from a 3D model (not including the render time), but the truth is that if you want to create a professional output, there is the need for more time and attention to detail. One way you can optimize the time it takes to go from point A to point B is by improving your workflow and trying some techniques that are used in real projects and that can be easily included in your standard workflow.

This first chapter is designed to cover the most important topics and gives you a solid foundation that will help you start working with Lumion. We will cover the following topics in this chapter:

- What it is possible to do with Lumion
- Where to get a demo version
- What do you need to work with Lumion
- Different Lumion versions
- Using additional models

- Keeping the project organized
- Using Lumion's layers
- The importance of materials
- Quick overview

The first few topics are aimed for those who are new to Lumion or don't know whether Lumion can meet their needs. For them, this initial section will work as an introduction. So, if you have some experience working with Lumion, feel free to jump to the section that most fits your need and before you skip this initial chapter, you may want to explore the last section called *Quick overview of Lumion* to check out the new interface and shortcuts in Lumion.

An introduction to Lumion for beginners

Lumion is targeted to produce visualizations and in most commercial projects this implies the use of a great deal of vegetation, a vast diversity of 3D models, a lighting system and materials, just to mention a few of the key aspects. Now, imagine having all of this information in real time. if you were to build a tree, not only will you see the materials, light, and shadows, but you can also move the camera around and see in real time how the tree looks like. As a plus, everything in Lumion is intuitive and user-friendly.

What is possible with Lumion

This creative independence and usability doesn't come without a fee because in order to provide this continuous feedback (real time), some corners need to be cut. This in turn affects how light is calculated and how materials are designed and react to light. Also, you need to keep a careful balance between 3D details and the amount of geometry used, as it is obligatory.

Lumion is not an application for producing photo-realistic renders. However, the simplicity and time it takes to have a final product ready to show to the client compensates for this lack of photo-realistic touch. You can see this for yourself at

`http://lumion3d.com/showcase/`.

So, what exactly is it possible for us to create with Lumion? Are we doomed to a low-quality product just because of some real-time technicalities? Let's have a look at the following render:

This image is a render taken from an example available in Lumion 5 and, hopefully, this can give you a good idea of not only Lumion's quality, but also the complexity that can be achieved in each scene. One thing that stands out in this render is the amount of 3D objects in the scene and you can take into consideration that individual trees along with the grass add loads of polygons to the scene. The truth is that Lumion can literally handle millions of polygons and this is useful not only for forest scenes such as the one we saw previously, but also for urban environments where we need a vast array of 3D models. Another key aspect that can be mentioned is the amount of 3D models available with Lumion (in particular, trees and plants), volumetric light, and mass placement that add life to a city scene with just a few clicks.

However, how do you know if Lumion is what you need for your company or for you pallet of tools?

Where to get a demo version, and some limitations of Lumion

Certainly, you are interested in trying Lumion to see whether it fits your needs, and the best solution to this is to try Lumion's free version. Great! A free version of Lumion! Nevertheless, I must warn you that although it's "free", this version is very and I repeat, very limited. You can use it to see how to import 3D models, check the 3D model's quality, and see how the material system work, but you will not have access to the most important and new features.

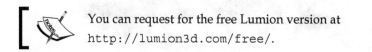 You can request for the free Lumion version at http://lumion3d.com/free/.

This demo version can help you check whether the workstation or computer can run Lumion and meet the minimum requirements. After launching Lumion for the first time, a benchmark is used to check your workstation to check whether there is a necessity to upgrade a hardware component in order to run Lumion more smoothly. To work with Lumion, you need a powerful workstation and in particular, a good graphic card which is the key hardware component in this equation. Have a look at the following requirements taken from Lumion's website.

The recommended system specifications are:

- A 64-bit Windows Vista, Windows 7 or Windows 8 OS
- 8GB RAM
- NVidia GTX 680 / AMD Radeon HD 7970 or a faster version graphic card with at least 2GB dedicated memory
- 7.5GB of free disk space

Does this mean you are doomed if you don't meet all the requirements? Not exactly! You may struggle to work with some scenes, but you can lower the viewport's quality, which in turn gives you more room to work. You can also make good use of the layers to hide some models of the scene, which in turn leaves more resources available for you. Nevertheless, it is when you render the scene that you may feel the biggest impact of not meeting all the requirements. A scene that could be rendered in 30 minutes with a good graphic card can take you a couple of hours with a lower-range graphic card. However, there are a few more things you should know about to have the full picture of what is involved when working with Lumion.

To find out which hardware will be best suited to working with Lumion, check out
`http://lumion3d.com/faq/#hardware`.

What is necessary to work with Lumion

An additional aspect you need to know is that Lumion wasn't designed with modeling and texturing in mind. Therefore, it is your responsibility to have a detailed 3D model and extra models if you don't like Lumion's optimized models. This means that all the modeling and texturing work needs to be done using an external software. If you are looking for something free, SketchUp is the best solution. Although, you can use Blender, which is a more complex and complete solution.

 You can find SketchUp at
`http://www.sketchup.com/products/sketchup-make`
and learn more about it at
`http://www.sketchup.com/learn`.
On the other hand, if you like to know more about Blender, visit
`http://www.blender.org/download/`.
You can learn more about it at
`http://www.blender.org/support/tutorials/`.

What about other applications? Well, you need to export the 3D models into a format that Lumion can read and import. To give you an idea of what Lumion supports, have a look at the following list:

- **Autodesk RealDWG**: `*.dxf`
- **Autodesk RealDWG**: `*.dwg`
- **COLLADA**: `*.dae`
- **FBX**: `*.fbx`
- **3ds Max**: `*.max`
- **3ds**: `*.3ds`
- **Obj**: `*.obj`
- **SketchUp**: `*.skp`
- **KMZ**: `*kmz`

Don't panic if you don't see your favorite application listed here, because it doesn't mean that Lumion is out of question. Most 3D applications can export the 3D model using the FBX or COLLADA file format. For example, I often use Revit for some projects and Lumion's team was kind enough to provide a free export for all users not only for Revit, but also for ArchiCAD.

If you are using Revit, have a look at `http://lumion3d.com/revit-to-lumion-bridge/`.

You can visit `http://lumion3d.com/archicad-tolumion-bridge/` if you are using ArchiCAD.

There are a few more things you need to know before jumping to Lumion's introduction.

Different Lumion versions

Lumion is available in 4 versions. We already saw that there is a free version of Lumion with loads of limitations and that the only purpose is to test some of the Lumion's features. You also have an educational version and the paid versions: Lumion Pro and Lumion.

What is the difference between these two versions? To answer that have a look at the following list:

- Output to real-time fly-through via Lumion Viewer
- Output of background music/sound in MP4
- Project files functionalities
- Content available

From all the points listed, the one that will have the biggest impact is the lack of content. Lumion only has a third of what is available in Lumion Pro and for someone who started working with Lumion, this could be a problem.

Do have a look at the full description of the differences between Lumion versions at

`http://lumion3d.com/products/`.

The good thing with the models that are bundled with Lumion is the fact that these 3D models are optimized to have quality and at the same time, are not too heavy in terms of geometry (which in turn makes your viewport slow). However, there is one way you can tackle this issue if you choose the standard Lumion version.

Using additional models

If you opt for the simpler Lumion version, the lack of content doesn't mean your project has to be empty and will lack diversity. You just need to start building your own library and if necessary, optimize the 3D model.

Where can we find good 3D models? The following is a list of some places where you can find free and paid models:

- **Creative Crash**: This model is available at `http://www.creativecrash.com/marketplace/3d-models`
- **Archive 3D**: This can be downloaded from `www.archive3d.net`
- **Mr Cad**: This can be obtained from `www.mr-cad.com`
- **3Delicious**: This is available at `www.3delicious.net`
- **TurboSquid**: This can be found at `www.turbosquid.com`
- **Resources Blogscopia**: This can be downloaded from `www.resources.blogscopia.com`
- **SketchUp Warehouse**: This can be downloaded from `http://sketchup.google.com/3dwarehouse/?hl=e`
- **Evermotion**: This is available at `http://www.evermotion.org/modelshop`

As was mentioned before, some of these models will need to be cleaned and optimized in order to have a balance between detail and geometry. How can we do this you ask? One way is to manually clean the geometry, which can be very tedious and time-consuming. On the other hand, you could use Simplygon. They have a free version that will give you enough room to start cleaning geometry.

> **Simplygon** automatically reduces the polygon count of 3D meshes primarily to create optimized models for visualization. For more information, refer to `https://www.simplygon.com/architecture-infrastructure`.

After this quick introduction to what is involved in working with Lumion, we can start and prepare ourselves to launch Lumion. However, the preparation starts before we even launch Lumion. How?

Keep your project organized!

From the CAD plans to the final image or animation clip, there is a lot of information that needs to be stored in an orderly way. You may prefer to work in a chaotic way, but it pays to be organized when using Lumion because similar to most applications, it uses links to files in order to work.

Lumion is not like 3ds Max or Maya where when you create a project, it automatically creates the list of folders to keep everything organized. This means that you will need to create some of these folders and keep the files inside those folders; otherwise, you could face some problems down the line. What would I recommend, you ask? Have a look at how the folders are organized in the following figure:

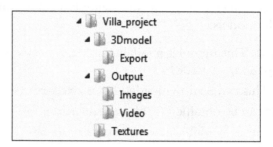

This is just an example of a way to organize the folders, but the significant bit is to keep it consistent. If you export the 3D model to a folder and save the textures in the same folder, this will prove useful later if there is a need to reload or reimport the 3D models.

There is an additional action you can take to keep your project organized and consequently, create a smooth workflow.

Using Lumion's layers

The layer's menu in Lumion is the simplest menu we can use but, initially, it may not be that easy to find. Firstly, it only appears when we have the **Import** and **Objects** menu selected and secondly, it is not that obvious as to where it is located. Do you see the black box with a number on the top left-hand side of Lumion's interface? That is the indication where the layers are, and once you move the mouse over this black box, the following options appear, as shown in the next screenshot:

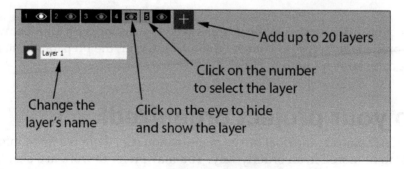

The workflow for using layers in Lumion is as follows:

1. Select the layer by pressing the number and if necessary, rename the layer.
2. Then, place the 3D model(s) on the scene, so that the model is placed inside the selected layer.

What happens if you add a model to a wrong layer? Nothing simpler than following the next steps:

1. Select the 3D model(s). The easiest way to do this is to hold the *Ctrl* key and then click on and drag with the left mouse button to draw a selection rectangle around the 3D model(s). An alternative way to do this is to hold the *Ctrl* key and then click on each 3D model's pivot.
2. With the 3D model(s) selected, chose the correct layer and click on the **Move selection to the layer** button, as shown in the following image:

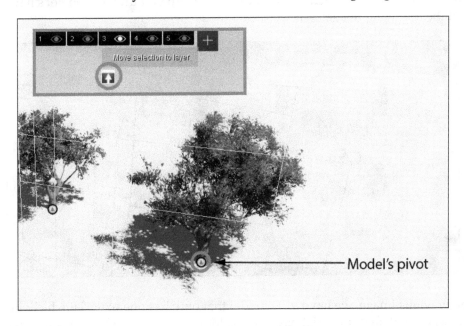

Make a good habit and practice in the way you use layers throughout the project. This not only makes your project more organized, but will also dramatically improve the speed of Lumion's viewport. How does it work? Well, every 3D model added to the scene means that Lumion needs to render that information in real time and that will decrease the speed of Lumion's viewport, which is measured in frames per second. The more **frames per second** (FPS) the more fluid working in Lumion will be, and you can see that information at the top-right corner of Lumion's interface.

So, how can the layers help us with this? During the process of building the 3D world in Lumion, we don't need to have all the 3D models on screen and in some situations, it is even better if we don't have them exposed. By using the layers to hide these 3D models, we not only reduce some visual noise, but we hide geometry, and hiding geometry means that Lumion has more resources available, which in turn makes the viewport much smoother.

One last thing that you need to understand before we start working with Lumion is why we need to use different materials on your models.

The importance of materials

This is something fundamental that needs to be done in order to work with Lumion. In simple terms, Lumion does not recognize your geometry, but instead recognizes the materials assigned to each surface or face. To help you understand, let's have a look at the following image:

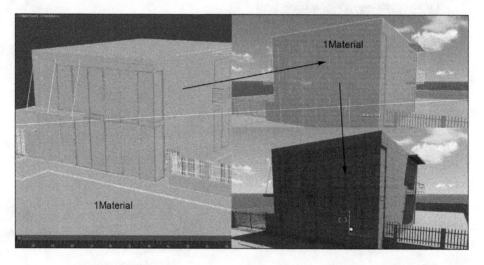

In the previous image, we have a 3D model that only has one material which, in this case, is the default material used by 3ds Max. So far so good, but watch what happens when we import the same model in Lumion and try to add a Lumion material. The image at the bottom-right corner shows the result of using only one material for the entire model — Lumion only recognizes "one big surface".

For that reason, you need to think ahead and identify which areas of your model need a specific material and you need to assign a different material for each section. As you can see in the following screenshot, it doesn't need to be something too fancy:

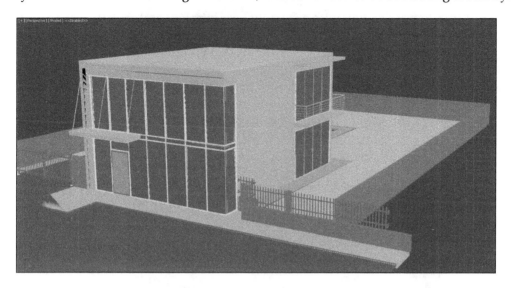

In this case, a simple colored material was applied to the different sections. For example, for the windows, we used a blue material; for the walls, a green material; and so on.

With all of these things in mind, you are now ready for a quick overview of Lumion and are ready to find out how it works. It is a crash course in two pages, but it will provide you with all you need to know to follow the rest of the book.

A quick overview of Lumion

As mentioned before, when you launch Lumion for the very first time, a benchmark starts to evaluate your workstation. After that comes the **Files** menu that is composed of five tabs—**New**, **Examples**, **Load scene**, **Save scene** (this tab only appears after you open a scene), and **Import full scene**.

The **New** tab is where you start a new project and here you can find nine different scenes to help you start working with Lumion. Keep in mind that the difference between each scene is the settings used for landscaping, weather, and lighting, which means that you can pick any scene available and then create the other eight scenes easily. Let's click on the **White** scene to start working with Lumion and explore the interface to see where we can find the main menus.

Exploring the interface and controlling the camera

Lumion tries to provide you with a friendly user interface and, initially, this may be confusing because you almost have no visual information and don't know where to find the menus. Lumion has four main menus that you can find on the left-hand side of the screen and when Lumion opens a new scene, the **Import** menu is the one that is opened by default. The other three menus only appear when you move the mouse close to the **Import** menu icon that you see on the screen. The following image shows you the toolbars that appear when you open each menu:

The next section that is essential is located on the right-hand side of the screen and here, you can see some small icons that give you access to different menus, as you can see in the following screenshot:

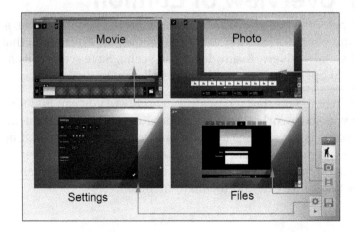

What essential information is missing here? How do you control the viewport and the camera? The easiest way to learn this is by having a look at the following screenshot:

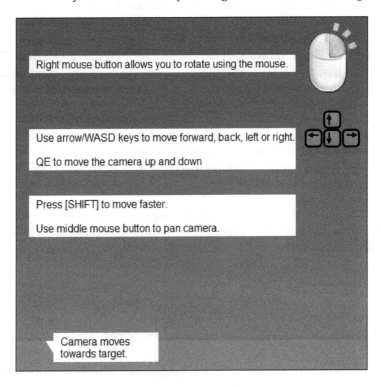

This information is available when you work with Lumion; you just need to hover your mouse over the **Help** button and all of these tips will appear. However, there are some shortcuts you can use to control the camera, which are as follows:

- Double-click with the right mouse button to zoom in
- Use the middle mouse button and move the mouse to pan the camera
- Scroll the wheel mouse up/down to zoom in and out of the camera
- *Ctrl* + *H* is used to reset the camera pitch to a horizontal viewpoint
- *O* + the right mouse button is used to orbit the camera

All of these shortcuts and keys that are used to control the viewport while working in Lumion will be used later to control and tweak the cameras used for the animation clip and to render images.

Summary

This first chapter was quick but essential introduction to Lumion. You saw what it is that we can do with Lumion regarding quality and also saw the complexity of the scenes you can create by adding literally millions of geometrical shapes. You learned that although a Lumion standard version doesn't provide the myriad of 3D models than Lumion Pro has, there are many places where you can find good quality models that will need some geometry cleaning, which don't compromise Lumion's speed.

The final section of the chapter was dedicated to the topic of how to start working with Lumion, starting with the right foot forward by keeping the project organized using Lumion's layers, and finally, we identified the need to use different materials when modeling. Now, after the crash course on how to start working with Lumion, you are ready for the next chapter.

The next chapter will help you with the next stage of the workflow: importing and controlling models. This may look straightforward, but can present some challenges that require the best practices to keep a smooth workflow.

2
Importing and Handling 3D Models

The complete collection of Lumion's features and their usability would be useless if we didn't have the capability to import our 3D models in Lumion. In the previous chapter under the section *What is necessary to work with Lumion*, we provided a list of all the file formats that Lumion can recognize and read. So, not only can Lumion import a wide variety of file formats, but it also has a good system to reload 3D models without losing the information attached to them, and by information we mean the materials assigned to the 3D models and their location. This is an important and crucial step in the entire workflow pipeline so let's have a look at what you are going to learn in this chapter:

- How to import 3D models
- Importing directly from SketchUp
- Importing 3d models from 3ds Max or another application using COLLADA or FBX
- Importing animations to Lumion
- Common problems and how to solve them
- Beginners' mistakes
- How to place 3D models in Lumion
- Randomness while placing objects
- The **Mass Placement** tool
- Controlling the 3D models
- Difference between model categories
- Importing large scenes
- Reloading imported files

As mentioned, importing 3D models is a crucial step because it allows you to check whether the 3D model has any geometrical problem that needs to be solved. Most of the time, if you use the COLLADA or FBX format, everything will work properly but you will still have some issues that cannot be easily spotted while modeling. Nevertheless, before we jump to such a technical section, let's see how we can import 3D models exported from several applications.

> If you prefer working on the landscape first, in case of an exterior scene have a look at *Chapter 4, Creating an Exterior Scene with Lumion*. There you can learn everything you need to know to sculpt and tweak the terrain to your needs.

Importing 3D models

When Lumion opens a new scene or loads a scene, the **Objects** menu is opened by default. This menu is what you have to use to and to start importing a 3D model, which you can import by clicking on the **Import** button and then selecting the **Add a new model** button, as shown in the following screenshot:

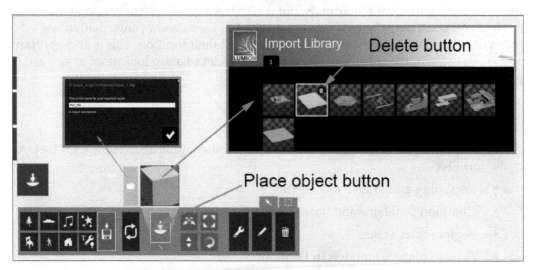

This screenshot provides some useful practices that you can apply from the beginning of your project. From the start, Lumion lets you rename the 3D model you are importing. This is really useful for the reason that you will probably import different versions of the same 3D model, particularly while working on a concept stage. This is also where you can decide to import simple animations along with the 3D model. As a best practice, you should start renaming and using layers from the start of your project.

As soon you click on the **Add to library** button, the place tool becomes available to start placing 3D models, which you can place by clicking on with the left mouse button. These models you import are stored in the **Import Library** button that you can access by clicking on the thumbnail above the **Place object** button. Here, you have the opportunity to delete or add the 3D model to a special category called **Favorites**.

> With time, you will import tons of 3D models that can be used in different scenes. The **Import Library** button is shared between scenes, so make good use of the **Toggle Favorite** option to select all those 3D models, such as trees and furniture, which you can easily recycle in different scenes.

Now that you know how to import a 3D model to Lumion, we we will cover not only how to import SketchUp files directly, but also how to import FBX and COLLADA files.

Importing SketchUp files

One of the greatest practices to work with Lumion is to use SketchUp for modeling and applying a basic texture. Firstly, SketchUp has a free version with a few limitations and is simple to use, and secondly Lumion can read SketchUp files. It may not seem important, but this feature simplifies your workflow by cutting out the middlemen. With SketchUp, you simply save the scene, import it into Lumion, and if necessary hit the **Reload** button to reimport the 3D model with the changes.

> Lumion may give you an error when you try to import a SketchUp file, but this is due to the fact that Lumion may not support some newer SketchUp versions. However, don't worry, as you can always "down save" a model to an older version.

Really, this is as simple as it can get. You may encounter some issues while importing SketchUp files which are common to all the formats and that is something we will see later in this chapter. For now, let's see two formats that work great in Lumion.

Importing from 3ds Max or other applications using COLLADA or FBX

We will make use of 3ds Max for this section but the same principles and settings can be used with other applications as well. The reason that only FBX and COLLADA are mentioned in this book is because they provide reliable results and therefore are the best to export complex scenes. This section is dedicated to showing you the settings that are recommended for FBX and COLLADA files.

Lumion gives you the opportunity to import 3ds Max files (.max), but Lumion's team still recommends COLLADA or FBX as your main file format. Do you want to know more about importing files in Lumion? Have a look at http://forum.lumion3d.com/importing/.

Here, you can find more information regarding applications, such as MicroStation, ArchiCAD, and Rhinoceros, just to mention a few.

You can also make good use of the forum if you find it difficult to achieve good results while exporting the 3D model from a specific 3D application. So, if Lumion supports other file formats, why use FBX or COLLADA?

Exporting settings for FBX files

The Autodesk FBX format is used to save 2D drawings and 3D geometry into a file that maintains full fidelity and functionality of the original file and that can be manipulated by multiple programs when you create interoperability between 3D applications.

However, FBX is not limited only to Autodesk products, which makes this file format a good candidate to export your 3D model. The following screenshot shows the settings that you need to correctly export the 3D model:

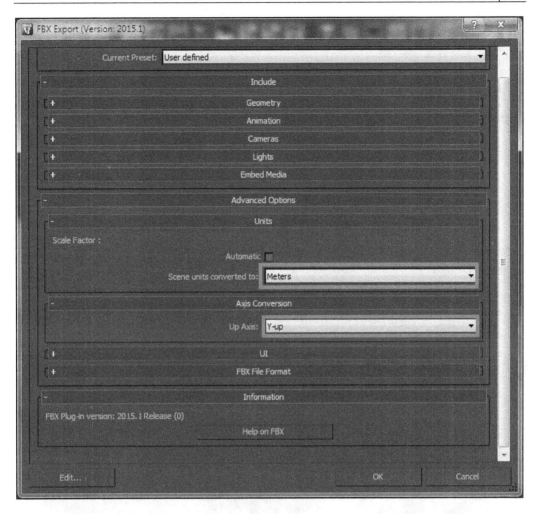

To export an FBX file, use the **Autodesk Media & Entertainment** preset and then change the settings under **Advanced Options**. Next, select the **Units** tab and choose **Meters** for the **Scene units converted to:** option. The final step is to make sure that **Up Axis** is set as **Y-up** and not **Z-up**.

Exporting settings for COLLADA files

The COLLADA file format is not something new and a reasonable number of 3D applications already supports this format. This is a great file format because it creates a bridge between the different 3D tools available, which include Lumion. However, you may ask, what are the benefits of using COLLADA instead of FBX?

The reason behind using the COLLADA file format instead of FBX or any other file format is that when you export the 3D model using COLLADA, it creates a folder with the textures used and at the same time has a low possibility of error.

Keep in mind that some Autodesk products have an option to export the 3D model as Autodesk COLLADA, but this option is not very stable and doesn't offer the same options you can get using OpenCOLLADA.

> You can download OpenCOLLADA from
>
> `https://github.com/KhronosGroup/OpenCOLLADA/wiki/OpenCOLLADA-Tools`.
>
> Here, you can find the plugin for 3ds Max and Maya.

After installing the plugin and when you export a 3D model, you can find the OpenCOLLADA (*.DAE) file format that you need. The settings needed are as follows:

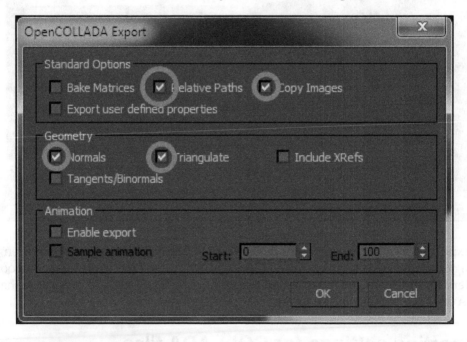

The **Copy Images** option is the one that will create a folder with all the textures inside and although this is not crucial, it is very useful and productive to have all of what you need in one location. However, does Lumion support animations? Find that out for yourself in the next section.

Exporting 3D animations

The answer to the previous questions is yes, Lumion supports animations. However, this support is very limited and controlling external animations is not that simple and stress-free. The animations you can import need to fulfill the following requirements:

- The frame rate should be set to 25 frames (PAL)
- Use FBX files or COLLADA but in case of the latest version, the interpolation between keyframes will be linear
- Lumion can only read move/rotate and scale keyframes which means you cannot import vertex animations, morph animations, or bone animations in this

Export the animation using the **Autodesk Media & Entertainment** preset (if you are using FBX) and while importing it in Lumion, don't forget to tick the **Import animations** option, as shown in the following screenshot:

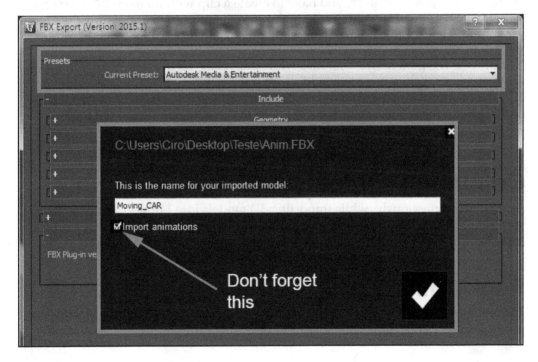

It's true that this limits us in terms of what we can accomplish in Lumion but there is still room for some basic animation that can help your scene.

There is another reason why animations in Lumion are not very practical and this is that once you import the animation, it will keep on playing as a loop. Imagine that you have a car moving in a straight line—here, the animation will keep on playing the same scene over and over again while you work. This can be annoying in particular when you have multiple animations in your scene, but things change once you move to the **Movie** mode.

 Don't forget to use layers to hide these animations. It will also improve the Viewport's speed.

The easiest way to explain this is with an example: let's say we have a car moving in a straight line and the animation lasts only for 30 seconds. Since you are using 25 frames per second, this means that this small animation covers 750 frames in those 30 seconds.

In order to use this animation, you have to create a clip with no more than 30 seconds or 750 frames. Why? The golden rule is: the clip's length needs to be equivalent to the animation's length; otherwise, the animation will keep on playing in a loop.

Now, things can go wrong sometimes while importing 3D models. There are some common issues that can be easily addressed but every now and then the solution may not be that obvious. In the next topic, you will learn some of the most common problems and the practical solutions not only to solve them but to avoid future problems as well.

Common problems and their solutions

As mentioned previously, while importing 3D models into Lumion, the process is very simple and most of the time you don't face any major issues. However, after the first few projects in Lumion, you will definitely learn how to avoid them.

Rookie mistakes

These are the issues that will crop up because you are new to Lumion but with practice, these can be reduced to a minimum.

The first issue arises when you import the 3D model that is placed on the scene. The difficulty here is that you don't see the model immediately. Why? One of the reasons is that you didn't create the 3D model close to the origin axis.

 The origin axis is the point where *X=0*, *Y=0*, and *Z=0*. Most of the 3D applications will represent this point with a red line for *X*, green line for *Y*, and blue for *Z*.

Every 2D and 3D application has a point called origin axis and Lumion uses this point as a reference to place the 3D model. If the 3D model is created where, let's say, *X=1000m*, *Y=1000m*, and *Z=0*, when it is imported you may get an image similar to this:

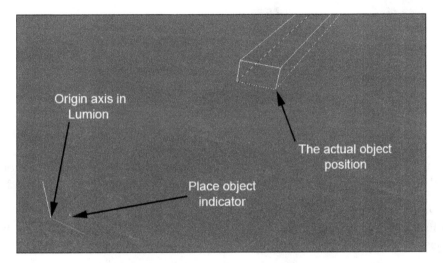

When you click to place the 3D model, which will be far from the location where you initially clicked. This may be something you want (we will see this later when you import large scenes) but if not, the solution is to move the objects close to the 0.0.0 point.

On the same line of thought—if you don't see the model, check the scale of the model and verify that you are using meters instead of centimeters or millimeters.

Reversed or missing faces

During the modeling process, it is common to end up with a few reversed faces. This may not be easy to spot on a 3D application but once the model is imported to Lumion, they disappear. In the following screenshot, you will see what happens with this extremely complex geometry:

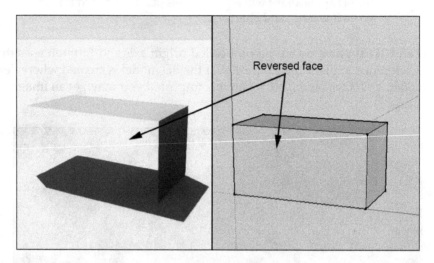

This is just an example to show you the impact of a reversed face. This situation is noticeable when you work on the exterior but keep an eye on strange shadows in the interior of your 3D model, where missing faces may not be so obvious.

The solution for this problem will depend on the 3D application you use. The best option is to do a quick search for how to reverse the face to normal.

So, what is next? The next subtopic will cover some common problems that you may encounter while working with Lumion. These are very specific errors and hopefully all your needs will be covered in the following subheading.

Most common importing issues

Let's start with some of the most common problems that you may face while importing 3D models:

1. **Problem**: When you import a 3D model, Lumion crashes.

    Reason: Keep in mind that Lumion has limits, so when you try to import a high - poly and complex model with loads of details, this can make Lumion slow and make it crash eventually.

Solution: The best way to solve this problem is to divide the model into sections and, further in this book, you can find the best practices to do this. Also, try to simplify the areas that are not visible in the camera.

2. **Problem**: After importing a model from Revit, the materials inside Lumion don't match.

   Reason: Some Revit materials are created using procedural textures or complex materials and cannot be converted to real-time materials. Lumion then tries to come out with the best representation based on base texture maps.

   Solution: The solution would be to stick to simple and basic materials and avoid procedural textures.

3. **Problem**: When you import a SketchUp file, Lumion crashes.

   Reason: An invalid texture duplication can make Lumion crash.

   Solution: Check the materials for any duplicates on textures and remove any characters, such as #, @, and & from the material and texture names.

4. **Problem**: While importing a file, objects shift out of place.

   Reason: When the file is exported, the internal relative position is not translated properly to world coordinates.

   Solution: Try to explode the 3D model because this will convert everything to world space coordinates.

5. **Problem**: When you import a 3D model with several objects inside, some don't appear in Lumion.

   Reason: Sometimes while modeling, we import a 3D model in the modeling package that we use and export everything to Lumion. It might happen that the 3D model we imported doesn't appear in Lumion.

   Solution: Try to explode the 3D models before exporting the 3D model.

6. **Problem**: After you reload a 3D model, a message appears informing you that there was an error while you imported the model.

   Reason: When Lumion doesn't have access to the drive of the original file, it gives this import error.

   Solution: You need to replace that file and while doing this, you need to set a new path for that file.

7. **Problem**: When you navigate to the 3D model, some surfaces might start to look strange.

    Reason: This can happen occasionally when the scene is so complex that it cannot be processed by the graphic card because it runs out of memory.

    Solution: Rebooting the PC can help you clean the memory of the graphic card. However, this also has to do with the number of polygons/3D points in the scene. Another possibility is that you have faces overlapping each other. Although the main solution is correct, with this issue inside the 3D modeling package, you can use the **Flicker Reduction** available in each material for a quick fix.

We only covered some of the most common situations so if you encounter something strange and none of the solutions work, the best course of action is to contact Lumion's team using the official forum. They always do their best not only to help you but, if necessary, create a hotfix for your problem.

Now that you know everything related to importing, let's see how we can place these 3D models in Lumion.

How to place 3D models in Lumion

We are by now familiar with the **Place object** button available in the **Objects** menu. So, why do you need to learn more about how to place 3D models in Lumion?

Firstly, don't forget to use layers as you learned in *Chapter 1, Getting Ready with Lumion 3D* under the section *Using Lumion's layers*. You are going to benefit from the use of layers at an earlier stage by keeping the project organized, and it will also help you when you shoot your movie.

Secondly, there are some tools that drastically improve the time it takes for you to place 3D models. Next, you will learn two great practices you can use while placing objects; in particular, when you need to place a lot of objects.

10 copies and different sizes

While placing any 3D model, before you click on the scene, you can press and hold the *Ctrl* and the *V* keys. The *Ctrl* key forces Lumion to place 10 copies but the *V* key creates these 10 copies with random sizes. This is a great way to add randomness to your scene and this attention to detail will make your scene more believable. After all, the world we live in is teeming with randomness where even two snowflakes are not equal.

There is a downside to this that you need to know: when you do this, you don't have control over the area where the 3D model is scattered. However, this downside is a great way to introduce the **Mass Placement** tool in the model.

Using the Mass Placement tool

This is a new tool that you can find on Lumion 5 and it should be included from version 1 because of the help it provides while working with the big scenes. This tool can pass unnoticed for the first time but you can find it under the **Place object** button, as shown in the following screenshot:

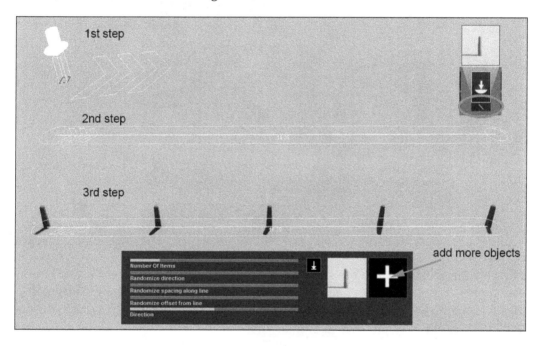

After selecting the 3D model from the library, click on the **Mass Placement** button that is under the **Place object** button. As you can see, you can now manipulate the 3D model and the three arrows that control the direction of the path. You have to click on the scene with the left mouse button, drag it, and then click on it again to define the length of the 3D model you need.

When you do that, a small box appears with several options that help you control how the object behaves on the path you traced. However, the best feature is the button with the big plus sign next to the object's thumbnail. This button lets you add more objects to the path and this gives you the freedom to create a very complex scene, as you can see in the following screenshot, where we used this path to scatter different species of trees and bushes:

The only thing that you need to keep in mind is that once you click on the **OK** button you cannot go back and tweak the settings, but if you click on the **Mass Placement** button, Lumion keeps the settings and the objects selected in memory in case you need them again.

> Trees and other plants are 3D models that can make the viewport struggle to keep so much information in real time. Press *F9* to show or hide high-quality trees and grass on the viewport.

So, let's move on to the next topic where you will learn a fundamental technique to work with external 3D models and Lumion's native 3D models.

Controlling the 3D models

So far so good but you need to move things around, and the best practice is to use shortcuts or hotkeys to improve the speed when you select 3D models. The keys to control the 3D model are:

- *M*: This is used to move the 3D model
- *L*: Press and hold this to scale the 3D model
- *R*: Press and hold this to rotate the 3D model's heading
- *P*: Press and hold this to rotate the 3D model's pitch
- *B*: Press and hold this to rotate the 3D model's bank
- *H*: Press and hold this to change the height in relation to the ground

Why is the move tool the only one that you don't need to press and hold? This is the tool that is selected by default so in order to access the other tools, you need to press and hold the corresponding key.

> Note that you can rotate the 3D model's pitch and bank only when you use the shortcuts.

However, before we jump to the additional best practices, there is something you need to know.

Using filters to select different categories

When working with Lumion, the **Objects** menu is where you can control all the 3D models, including those you import. Managing large scenes can be challenging sometimes because of all the 3D objects in the scene but, inside the **Objects** menu, you can control the 3D models using two different modes, as shown in the following screenshot:

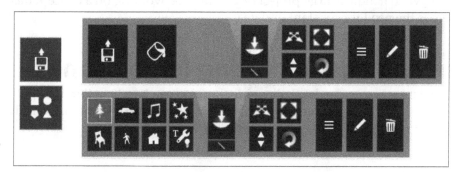

The **Place** mode is where you have access to all the libraries and the possibility to import an external 3D model. However, when you need to control all the different 3D models, things can be confusing. Why? Let me show you why with the use of an example, and for that you need to:

1. Open the **Objects** menu.

2. Select the **Nature** category (the first) and place the tree that is selected by default.

3. Select the **Transport** category (the second) and place the boat that is selected by default.

If you follow these steps, the **Transport** category is selected and this means that you can move, rotate, or delete the boat. However, try now to do the same thing with the tree. This will not be possible because you don't have the correct category selected but there is a dirty trick you can do to quickly move and rotate the 3D models around even if they are not from the same category.

This is a good practice that you can use all the time and it is really simple: press the *F12* key and with the left mouse button, select the object—now you can move the object around. If you need more control, then the best thing to do is to select the appropriate category. Don't forget to press the *M* key to deactivate the *F12* option.

However, now you have the **Move** mode that goes against all that we mentioned before. With this mode, every model can be selected and controlled independent of their category. To help you with this task, the **Filter** feature needs to be used so that you don't accidently change certain 3D models. The workflow is very simple, click on each category you don't want to change and they are ignored by Lumion. In the preceding screenshot, only the **Import** category was selected because we only wanted to control the imported 3D models.

Before we close this chapter, there are a few things you need to learn. After all, you will not be working with small houses in every single project. Time will come when you will have to handle a large project or you may be working on a concept design and there is the need for constant updates.

Handling and importing large scenes

Importing larges scenes can be challenging. Lumion can handle millions of polygons but importing a large amount of geometry in one go can crash Lumion. Consider the project shown in the following screenshot:

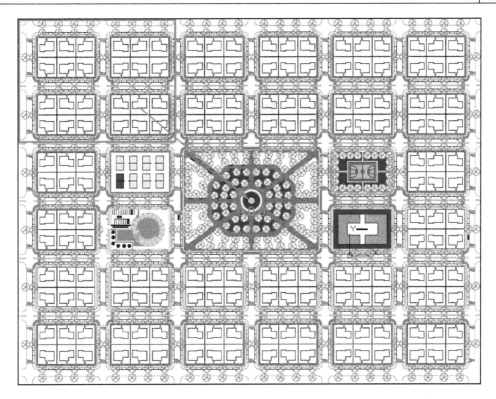

Each small rectangle has six houses on it and in the middle we have a nice park surrounded by other buildings. If you try to import so much information in one go Lumion will crash, so you need to "break" the geometry into small sections, as shown in the preceding screenshot. The rectangle shows how we divided the geometry into smaller sections but how can you import all of this geometry and assemble everything together?

The best workflow is to break the geometry into different sections. Don't move the geometry to the 0.0.0 point and export each section individually. Import everything to Lumion and don't worry where you are placing the object. Now select the **Move** mode in the **Objects** menu and select **3D model** option imported and this will activate the window with the **X**, **Y** and **Z** coordinates, as you can see in the following screenshot:

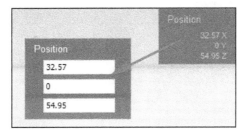

This window appears next to the **Move** mode panel and once you hover the mouse over it, the window allows you to insert values. If you insert a value of **0** in each box, you will start seeing each section being moved to the correct section it belongs to.

Updating 3D models in Lumion

What happens if, after you import a 3D model, a few changes are made? Do you have to import the 3D model again, tweak materials, and recheck the correct location? The answer is No—thanks to **Context menu** option. When you select **Context** and click on **3D model** you can access three submenus, as you can see in the following screenshot:

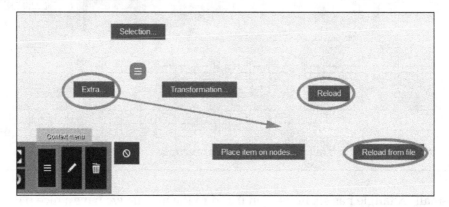

A click on the **Extra** submenu gives you access to two important options: **Reload** and **Reload from file**.

If you change the 3D model and export it to the same folder with the same filename, you can hit the **Reload** option and the 3D model will be reimported. On the other hand, if you export the 3D model with a different filename, you need to click on **Reload from file** which in turn opens a window where you can navigate to the new file to replace the current model.

As you can see, reloading and reimporting 3D models in Lumion is as easy as this. However, you will learn in the next chapters how to make good use of this tool.

Summary

Another milestone was achieved with this chapter. Here, you learned that importing 3D models, although a simple task, needs to follow some rules. You saw how to not only import 3D models directly from SketchUp but also how to use FBX and COLLADA files. Nothing is perfect and sometimes importing 3D models in Lumion can cause some problems, but you learned the most common issues and how to tackle them. Keep in mind the rookie mistakes to avoid the most common modeling issues.

After this, you learned how to place 3D models but, most importantly, you learned how to place several copies of a 3D model and even how to scatter them across a line path. Don't forget that there is a difference between external 3D models and Lumion's native ones. The final section showed you the best practices to import large scenes and how to update 3D models already imported in Lumion.

The next chapter is going to be a more practical one, where you will learn some of the best practices to create and optimize interior scenes in Lumion. We will cover Lumion's objects and their properties, principles to create materials, and the best techniques to improve light and shadows.

3
Creating an Interior Scene with Lumion

In this chapter, we will introduce you to some efficient techniques for creating an interior scene with Lumion. Primarily, Lumion was developed to create exterior renders and even with more recent versions, you will see that Lumion has more content for exterior scenes. However, the interior scenes are easier to create and with some attention to detail, it is possible to produce very believable 3D renders. Some of the most important aspects of working with interior scenes are attention to detail and lights. In particular, regarding lights, it pays to learn how we can use them to sculpt the environment. Volumetric lighting and global illumination are just two features that we can use to drastically improve the final output, but we will cover those in *Chapter 7, Producing a Still Image with Lumion*.

The topics we will explore in this chapter are as follows:

- Adding details to the 3D model
- Lumion 3D model libraries
- Balancing the use of 3D models
- Using the **Context** and **Edit Properties** menus
- Editing the **3D model** properties
- Materials
- Working with lights
- Improving interior lighting with the fill light
- Difference between shadows
- Editing light's properties

However, before we begin, keep in mind that your goal should not to be to copy what we do here, but instead your goal should be to apply the techniques that you will learn here in your own projects.

Checking and refining the 3D model

It doesn't matter if a client provides a 3D model or you use a model you created, you still need to check whether there is any bad geometry and, most importantly of all, the level of detail.

The level of detail

The level of detail that is required depends on two aspects. The first aspect you need to take into consideration is how close the 3D model is to the camera? Something that will be in the foreground will need to be more detailed than another 3D model that is, perhaps, in the back of the room hidden by a curtain. It sounds really basic and like a simple tip, but the most efficient practices tend to be simpler.

You will have several benefits if you take this first practice into consideration. You won't have to spend time modeling details that are not visible or have no visual impact on the final render. Since you'll have fewer polygons, the scen51e will be lighter and faster to render. However, what is the second aspect that constrains the level of detail?

For that I need to ask whether you are producing a video or an image. Why? A still image needs more care and attention to detail because your eyes have nowhere to go. You are stuck with a single frame and all your attention is focused on that image. So, the level of detail you need for a video is usually lower because you only have a few seconds before the camera moves to another point.

Adding additional 3D models

While working with interior scenes, it is always a good habit to check references. You can use the Web, but also, you can make good use of architectural magazines and observe not only what the scene contains, but also how the photographer has chosen to compose the shot.

If you are trying to reproduce a room where people are supposed to live, what do you need? Small details are sometimes overlooked, such as electrical switches and plugs. What about skirting and coving as final touches to your scene? In this matter of detail, there is something you must not forget.

Beveling edges

This topic might seem cliché, but the truth is that beveling edges has a big impact on how realistic your render looks. Why such impact? Nothing in this world has razor sharp edges, even things made by man, and for that reason, beveled edges are part of our daily life. When you bevel the edge of a surface, you allow this edge to capture highlights that help you sell the render as real. Have a look at the following screenshot to understand this:

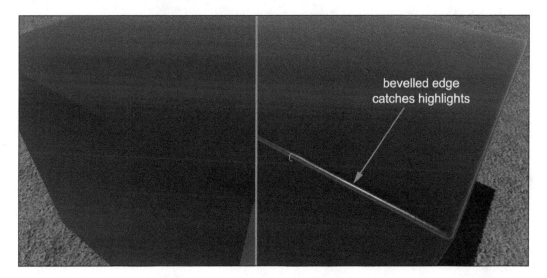

Which cube looks more natural and realistic? The only difference between the two cubes is the beveled edges and it is amazing to see how something so simple has such a big impact on the realism of your scene.

Once you have finish checking all of these key aspects, you will probably want to start populating your scene with some content. This is a good cue for us to now introduce you to the Lumion 3D model libraries.

A quick overview – Lumion's native 3D models

The Lumion version you have bought will constrain what you have available in each library. The following list gives you a good overview of what is available in Lumion Pro:

- **The nature library**: As you can see in the following screenshot, in this library, you will find more than trees. The **Clusters** tab is a lifesaver for when you need to fill the landscape with loads of trees. Since they are far away from the camera, the clusters of trees Lumion provides are good enough to fill the scene.

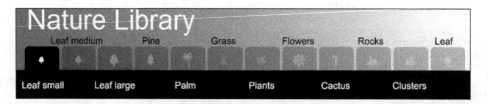

- **The transport library**: This library encompasses all sorts of transport, including railway and air transport, which you can see in the following screenshot:

- **The sound library**: Usually, this library is used later in the project when you want to add nice touches and bring life to your scene using the sounds provided in Lumion. This is not the only way to use sounds in Lumion because there are some effects you can use as well.

- **The effects library**: This library gives an added touch to your project by providing some particle simulation, as shown in the following screenshot:

- **The indoor library**: In this library, you can find a good variety of 3D models, but it is highly recommended that you use some extra 3D models to fill the gaps that you will eventually find out about. Here is the screenshot of the indoor library:

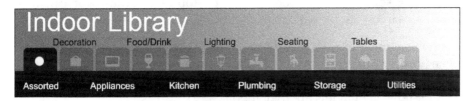

- **The people and animals library**: This library gets better with time. Although the name of the library mentions animals, the reality is that you don't have much variety in this. As you can see in the following screenshot, you not only have 3D models here, but also 2D models that include silhouettes:

- **The outdoor library**: Some of the most useful models can be found under the **Lighting**, **Furniture**, and **Utilities** tabs. The **Buildings** tab is a great one for filling the scene around your building.

- **The lights and utilities library**: This is a great library for interior scenes. The **Spotlights** tab gives a preview of each spotlight, helping you decide on the best lighting for your living room.

All this information sounds great now, and perhaps you may be thinking, if I knew I had this 3D model, I wouldn't have wasted time modeling one. Well, if you create a PDF document with screenshots and all the 3D models available, this will definitely help you. This is something that doesn't need to stop here because you can also incorporate this into your own 3D models.

Then, at the beginning of each project, you can view the catalogue of 3D models to determine how much time you have available and how much time you can save. However, now that you have had a closer look at what is available in Lumion, you may wonder if the 3D models are that good.

Balancing Lumion's models with external models

Best practices are not only about techniques, but also about good decisions. If you had an opportunity to have a closer look at the models, you would probably have noticed that some of them don't look so good when they are closer to the camera.

The reason for this is because Lumion is a real-time engine that needs all the resources available to allow real-time feedback. For that reason, they have had to optimize the 3D models and this optimization meant that they created 3D models with low geometry and added details using textures.

This means that if you want to create believable renderings, you need 3D models with far more details closer to the camera. The following screenshot shows you the difference between a Lumion 3D model and an imported 3D model:

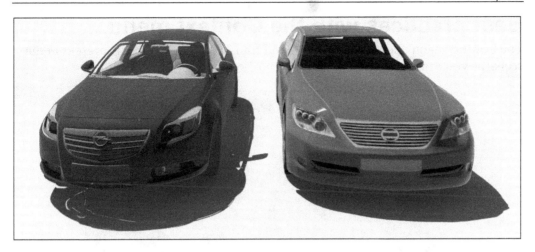

Of course, all this detail that you see on the car to the left comes with a cost: the frames per second on the viewport drops and the render will take longer as well. That is why you need to balance the use of 3D models. If the model is close to the camera, you will benefit from more details, but if the model is away from the camera, you may manage with a low geometry model.

Populating the scene with 3D models

What 3D models did you use in your scene? Most importantly, how did you place them? In this example, we will populate the interior of a coffee shop, and could start with the tables, as shown in the following screenshot:

After creating a layer for furniture, you can use the **Mass Placement** tool to place the row of tables. However, what if, after clicking on the **OK** button, you realize that for the sake of realism, the tables could have some variation? Do you have to select the tables one by one and then delete them? Not exactly.

Best practices with the Context menu

The **Context** menu allows you to select and transform the 3D models present in the scene, as you can see in the following screenshot:

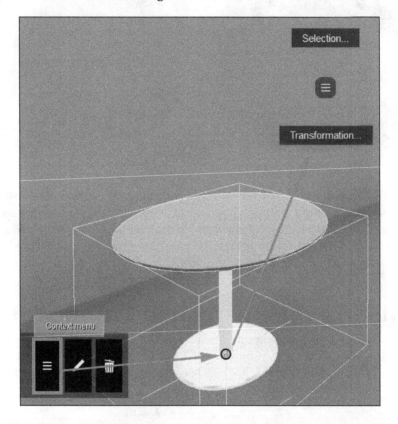

The **Selection** submenu is one of the best features you can find in Lumion and you should make a habit of implementing it in your workflow. When you click on this menu, the following options are made available to you:

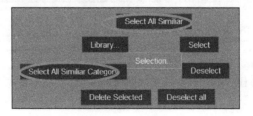

Since we want to select all the tables we previously placed, the best option you can select for this is the **Select All Similar** option. This will ensure that you only select every single instance of this 3D model.

What about the **Select All Similar Category** option? The word category should give you a hint to understanding what is possible with this feature. Let's consider a plausible situation where you need to select all the furniture of a living room. The **Select All Similar** option wouldn't work properly in this situation because we have a vast array of 3D models, but **Select All Similar Category** selects all the 3D models that fall under a certain category or library, which will help you to quickly organize your scene into layers.

In our scene, we used the **Select All Similar** option to quickly select the tables and then we deleted them using the **Trash object** button. The reason why we are doing this is because we need to add some randomness to the tables in order to create a believable scene.

The two options you can keep in mind while working with **Mass Placement tool** are: **Randomize spacing along line** and **Randomize spacing from line**. The next step is to add some chairs around the tables.

Rotating the 3D models with the mouse – the rotate option

While placing the 3D models in the scene, you probably noticed that 3D models keep the same orientation, which in some cases, such as the case of placing chairs around the table, doesn't produce the nicest results. However, as you can see in the following screenshot, there is a quick solution to this problem as well:

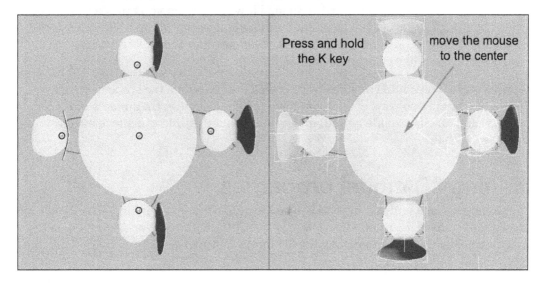

In this case, select all the chairs and select the **rotate heading** tool from the toolbar. Press and hold the *K* key while you move the mouse so that the object faces the mouse.

Also, if you are not happy with the result, click on the **Undo** button that appears next to the toolbar, as you can see in the following screenshot:

This button only appears when you make certain changes, such as moving an object, but don't forget that you can only undo your last action.

Now that we have the four chairs with the correct orientation, does this mean we have to repeat the process for each individual table? Let's have a look at the following section.

Duplicating 3D models with the Alt key

The *Ctrl* key selects the 3D models you need, which in this case, will be the four chairs. After selecting the **Move object** tool, you need to press and hold the *Alt* key to duplicate the objects while moving them. However, when you approach a table, it may be difficult to place the chairs without placing them on top of the table. To overcome this issue, just press and hold the *Shift* key and this will constrain the movement to keep the chairs at same height.

Alternatively, you could copy the table as well and populate the scene using this technique, but in one way, even if you have to spend some extra minutes placing the chairs, this will provide a randomness that is not possible to achieve even if you adjust each chair.

Editing 3D model properties

Populating a scene with 3D models is a task that needs some thinking about and time in order to achieve a natural look. There is an additional way to add uniqueness to your scene and that is by tweaking the 3D model's properties.

For example, you might have noticed that every time you place a car, each new car has a different color. Actually, the color shown in the library is red, but you hardly get a red car. This is because almost every 3D model in Lumion has some properties that you can change; this helps to make each project unique. Best of all, you can change these properties on multiple 3D models.

For the example in this chapter, some tables and chairs were added, but the look we get is too dull because every chair and table is white. For this interior scene, we need some color to bring cheerfulness to the place and for that, we use the **Edit Properties** menu.

You can find this menu located on the toolbar if you go to the **Objects** menu, as shown in the following screenshot:

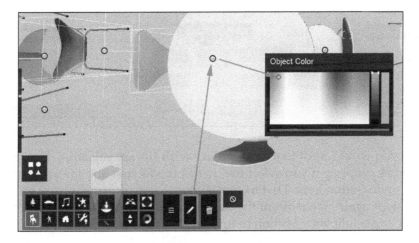

The workflow is simple—select the object (or multiple objects) and click on the **Edit Properties** menu. When you select the object pivot, this opens a new window where you can edit the object; in this case, the chair's color.

The options you have available with the **Edit Properties** menu will change according to the type of your 3D model. For example, you can change the color of a tree, but there are no options available for people.

Now, back in our example, we just realized that by mistake, the wrong table was used. This may not sound like the worst case scenario, but we will lose some time correcting this error, or perhaps not.

The Replace with library selection option

The best practice to solve a problem like this is very simple. Go to the library and select the correct table. Then, use the **Context** menu to select all the tables with the **Select All Similar** option. Open the **Context** menu again and this time, select the **Library** option, as shown in the following screenshot:

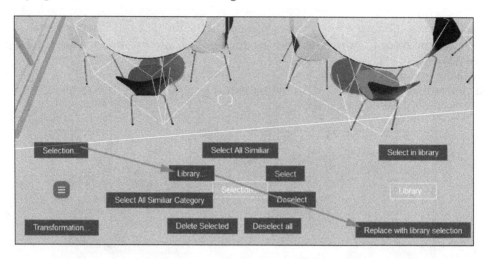

The option you would want to use is **Replace with library selection**. However, this will only work properly if you select the correct model first and for some reason, there is no undo button here. That means if you do this incorrectly, you will need to repeat the steps again. What about the **Select in library** option? Good point. Let's have a look at the following section to find out the answer.

Using the Select in library option

While working with complex scenes, it can be difficult to recognize the type of model you have used for the scene. This is most difficult when working with vegetation and when you want to associate a tree in the scene with the thumbnail in the library. Using **Select** in the library option, you will be able to select the 3D model, but you still need to open the library and select the correct tab to see the model highlighted, as shown in the following screenshot:

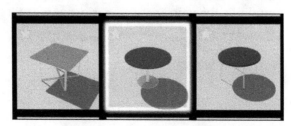

Sometimes, it can be difficult to see the halo around the 3D model, but a quick look at the thumbnail above the **Place object** tool will give you a helping hand.

After placing the 3D models, the next step could be the materials. So, let's see what is available for interior scenes.

A quick overview – Lumion's physically based materials

What exactly does physically based materials mean and what is the impact of this on your scene? Physically based materials mean that the material will actually react to light in the correct way and not how we intuitively think it should react. The end result is more accurate and typically looks more natural.

 If you want to learn more about this subject, have a look at `https://www.allegorithmic.com/pbr-guide`. Allegorithmic have created two guides for the theory and practical of physically based renderings.

Materials are an essential factor for producing believable renders and Lumion's team have done a great job by providing more than 600 materials that can serve as a base for your scene.

 The materials were designed to be used on the 3D models you imported. You cannot apply these materials to Lumion's native 3D models.

The **Materials library** is divided into logical sections, as you can see in the following figure:

The process for applying the materials is simple: select a surface and then select a material. If you are not happy with the material, select the surface and simply change the material. Since Lumion 5, the interface has been more intuitive and simpler, as you can see in the following screenshot:

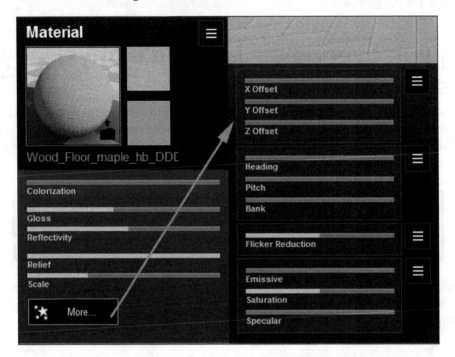

The **More** option let's you choose more advanced parameters that help you tweak the texture to the way you want it to be and the way it reacts to light.

What are the best practices for working with materials in Lumion? In reality, you have three options for working with materials in Lumion:

- The first option is to use the imported materials that you can create on your favorite modeling application
- The second option is to use Lumion's materials
- The third option is to create materials using Lumion's Standard material

The first and third options are very similar, in that you need to create your own textures and assign them to the correct surfaces, which probably involves some UV unwrapping.

However, it doesn't matter which option you use because eventually, you need to tweak the materials within Lumion. So, what are the things you need to keep in mind while tweaking the materials? Let's have a look at this in the following sections.

Small adjustments

One basic and essential adjustment you need to make concerns the texture's scale. Most of the materials that you applied to the surface will need this adjustment and some parameters that can help you with this you are **X offset**, **Y offset**, and **Z offset**, **Heading**, **Pitch**, and **Bank**. You can find these options when you click on the **More** button.

Colorization is not the same as **Saturation**. With colorization, you can completely remove the color of the texture, while the **Saturation** option increases the intensity of all the colors in the material.

Finally, the **Relief** option works as a bump feature. Each material in Lumion has a normal map and this can be tweaked (using the **Relief** option) to modify how light reacts to the surface. The material editor automatically creates a relief definition for imported diffuse images, which saves time.

These are some essential adjustments you need to perform to create a believable material. Just because the material has a specific look, that doesn't mean you cannot twist it to meet your needs. Let's explore some useful options.

Reflection and glossiness – make it believable

Reflection and **glossiness** are two settings that are used to tweak the way the material reacts and how it reflects the light. They are essential if you want your material to look realistic. The **Reflection** option is the most obvious because if we increase this setting, the surface becomes more reflective. There isn't much we can add on this subject, but what about glossiness? Let's have a look at the following section to get the answer.

Controlling the reflection sharpness

The **Glossiness** setting is one that can be used to define how sharp the reflections are. With the **Glossiness** setting, you can tweak the uniformity of the surface (by adding small defects) and this can create a very shiny surface with sharp reflections or a blurry reflection.

While working with **Reflection** and **Glossiness**, you can use the **Specular** option to balance the effect. Knowing this is great, but what are exactly the best values to use on my material? The answer is very simple: there aren't any. The simple fact is that if you want to make a material believable, you need to compare the material not with what you think is right, but with references. In the beginning, this can be very frustrating because we all like to think that there is a secret formula for a perfect material, but through observation and the use of references, you can create realistic materials. However, there is an additional way to control how light reflects on the surface and that is by using the alpha channel.

Controlling reflections with the alpha channel

This option only works when you import an image as a texture for the material. The alpha channel needs to be created using an image editor, such as Photoshop or GIMP, and you can use it to store grayscale images. As you can see in the following screenshot, this information has a massive impact on how the surface reflects light:

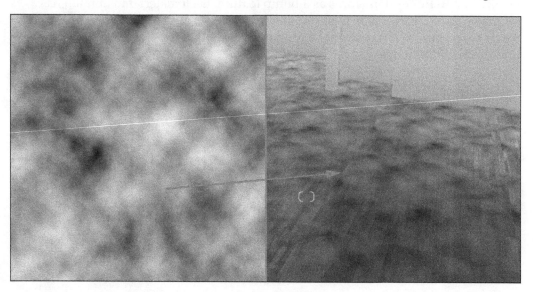

In other 3D applications, this map is called a reflection map and can be based on your main texture. A quick way to create one is by desaturating the image and using it as a reflection map.

However, as mentioned before, you don't have to rely only on Lumion's materials. You can create your own textures and use them in Lumion with the **Standard** material. Now, we can move on to another equally important section that involves the use of lights to create believable interior scenes.

Working with lights for interior scenes

It is not difficult to perceive that Lumion's main goal is to produce exterior renders, but we have available tools that help you produce good interior renders. You have lights, global illumination, volumetric effects, and a new feature called **Hyperlight**.

However, let's start with the **Lights and special objects** menu, where you can find all the Lumion interior lights.

Placing a spotlight, omni light, or fill light

If you open the **Lights and special objects** menu, you will be presented with three tabs, but for now, you only need the first and second tab with the spotlights and fill light.

The process is very simple. You select a light and place the light on the scene just like you do when placing a 3D model, as you can see in the following screenshot:

When you place the light, you need to hold the left mouse button and move up to set the height of the light. This works fine in a situation when the light needs to be pointing down, However, what if you need the light pointing to a specific object?

If you access the **Light** properties using the **Edit Properties** menu, you can see a small icon, as shown in the following screenshot:

Click on this button to access a mode where you can left click in order to control where the light points to. Once you finish, click on the **OK** button to save the new position.

However, as you can see in the previous screenshot, the control you have over the light doesn't end here. You can tweak the light's intensity along with the **Cone Angle** option that constrains the area that is illuminated by the spotlight. Use the **Show light source** option to mimic the glare and overexposed area that a real light would create.

Difference between lights

What is the difference between a spotlight, an omni light, and a fill light? A **spotlight** comes from theatre lighting and projects a bright beam of light, and the area that is affected by the light is controlled using the cone's angle. The **omni** and **fill** lights are very similar and the only difference between them is the intensity. This light emits light equally in all directions, or as the name suggests, fills the area with uniform lighting. Some practical applications of this light include lamp posts.

While placing lights in our scene, it is important to remember that the more lights we have in the scene, the longer the render will take. So, you need to think carefully about how many lights you really need. It is a fact that the light you get from a spotlight may not be sufficient to light the entire room, but you can use the fill light to help you with this.

A fill light creates good and uniform illumination for the entire room, but it doesn't produce any shadows. Keep these things in mind because in *Chapter 7, Producing a Still Image with Lumion,* you will see how to use the global illumination effect and the **Hyperlight** feature to drastically improve the lighting in a scene.

Before we finish this chapter, there is something you need to tweak to create an optimized interior scene.

Shadows – accuracy, speed, and memory modes

You might have noticed while placing a spotlight the shadows that it produces, but as soon you finish placing the light, the shadows disappear.

 If you need to check the shadows produced by a light or a set of lights, select them by pressing and holding the *Ctrl* key and select each one to see the shadows produced by that particular light.

There is nothing wrong with your scene; instead, Lumion is trying to save memory by not showing the shadows. The shadow quality is controlled using the **Light Properties** window, where you can find the following options:

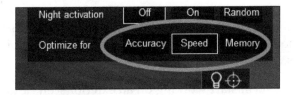

In order to improve the render time, we need to have a balance between the shadow details and quality. The following screenshot shows the comparison between the three different shadow options:

To get a better perception of how the shadows look, do a render before taking any artistic decisions. The viewport only gives you a rough idea.

With the **Accuracy** option, the shadows created by the spotlight are updated in every single frame, or in other words, the shadows produced are in real time. These shadows also look more realistic and sharp because a 2048 x 2048 pixel shadow texture is used to create a very accurate and detailed shadow.

The **Speed** option provides the perfect balance between render time and shadow quality because it only uses a static 512 x 512 pixel texture and the shadows produced are not in real time.

Finally, the **Memory** option only uses a static 128 x 128 pixel texture, but the shadow quality turns out to be very low.

Summary

Details, good models, and perfect lighting are the key points you should remember from this chapter. In this chapter, you learned that you need to pay close attention to details since interior scenes need more work for them to be believable. You saw the comparison between Lumion's models and external models and how this level of detailing can have a big impact on your scene. After learning some best practices for placing and populating a scene, you were introduced to Lumion's physically based materials and to another key aspect that helps you produce good interior scenes: lights and shadows.

In the next chapter, we will start working on an exterior scene and see some of the best practices for creating complex scenes. This includes the use of the **Landscape** menu. In the next chapter, we will also explore several ways to create complex terrains in Lumion with the help of sculpt tools and heightmaps.

4
Creating an Exterior Scene with Lumion

Each type of project has challenges, and when working with exterior scenes this is no different. Light and shadows are covered by the exterior lighting system, but you still need to plan the best way to approach an exterior scene. Are we talking about a massive urban environment or a complex landscape? Are we preparing a still image or an animation? These are only a few examples of the several aspects that need to be kept in mind while working with Lumion, because there are different tools that can be used in each situation.

In this chapter, you are going to learn the best practices for working with the **Landscape** menu to achieve the following:

- Planning your scene
- The **Merge scene** feature
- The **Landscape** menu
- Landscape types
- Creating coast and valley scenes
- Creating rivers and ponds
- Using the **Height** and **Terrain** submenus
- Working with heightmaps
- Tools for creating heightmaps
- Imported terrains and the landscape material
- Creating a lawn using the **Grass** menu
- Tweaking texture using the **Paint** menu

Let's start with the most important step needed to produce exterior scenes planning.

Planning your scene

Exterior scenes need time to be planned if you want to minimize any issues and have a smooth workflow. Although you may be working with small buildings in some situations, you still need to plan ahead how to build the scene.

One of the first things you have to check is whether the client wants a still image or an animation. Why? For one, with a still image, you don't have to worry too much about what is behind the camera and you may only have to add some geometry to be reflected on the windows. However, when working with an animation, the camera may move to a position where you need to add some objects; otherwise, it will be just an empty green field.

On the other hand, just because you are working with an animation, you cannot simply fill the scene with everything in terms of 3D models to Lumion. Your workstation has limits, and the same applies to Lumion. You can obviously work with layers, but there is something else that can help you work with big and complex scenes.

The Import, Export, and Merge scene features

Handling massive and complex scenes can be challenging, not only because of the amount of information in the scene but also because Lumion's viewport can struggle to present so much information.

Let's consider the example showed in the following screenshot:

For this project, the client only wanted some still images of the house in the centre, and because this was an urbanization, all the houses would be the same with some differences in the exterior materials.

The most logical first step was to divide the scene into blocks with six houses, export all of the blocks, and use the coordinate system to place them in the correct positions. However, because of the camera's position, you can still see some of the houses around the main subject. That means we had to fill the space with the same house, trees, vegetation, and so on.

Although possible, it is not very practical and easy to copy six houses with all of that information and place it on each block around the main subject.

> Remember that you can move and duplicate an object or multiple objects using this combination: **Move** tool + *Shift* + *Alt*. The *Shift* key keeps the same height while moving.

This is when **Import full scene** and **Export full scene** comes to the rescue. When you go to the **Files** menu, you can see these two tabs, as shown in the following screenshot:

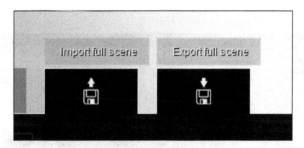

The first step in this workflow is to prepare one block of six houses with all the detail we need. Similarly, you may find it useful to divide or break the scene into smaller and lighter scenes that give you the ability to easily move around and tweak the 3D models.

Then you need to export every single scene using the **Export full scene** tab. This gives you the opportunity to save a file with the LS5 extension. Think of this process as creating references that you can assemble into a single scene.

To import the scenes you export, use the **Import full scene** tab. Here you can find two options, as shown in the following screenshot:

The **Import Scene…** option, although it allows you to import the entire scene, is not the best option. Why? Because it doesn't give you the freedom to choose what to import, as the **Merge Scene…** option does.

The following screenshot shows the options available with the **Merge Scene…** option:

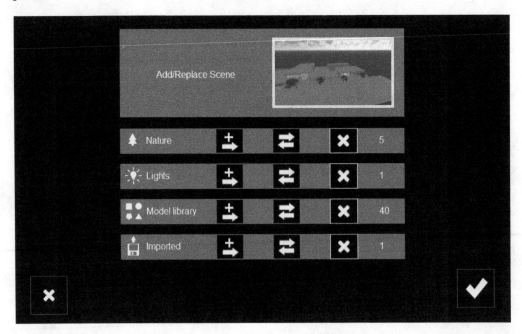

As you can see, the nature of this feature is far more complex, but at the same time, more flexible than the **Import Scene...** option. The scene you want to merge is divided into four sections: **Nature**, **Lights**, **Model library**, and **Imported**.

The three buttons next to each category allow you to control what is imported or updated, as shown in the following diagram:

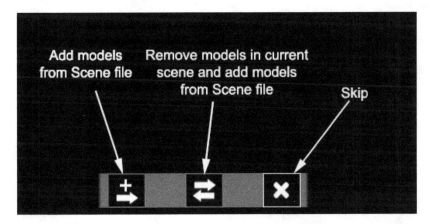

Now you can see why using this technique is one of the best practices for keeping the workflow smooth and problem-free. Lumion even creates another scene called **Import as a backup**. One word of caution: use layers to control each scene you import or merge, or it will be very difficult to handle all the files.

Another best practice when producing exterior still images or animations is the use of the **Landscape** menu to control the terrain and textures.

Quick overview – the Landscape menu

When working on an exterior project, the landscape has a big impact on any scene. Landscape refers to all the visible features of an area of land and includes things such as rivers, ponds, roads, animals, and vegetation.

The **Landscape** menu deals with some of the aspects just mentioned that create a beautiful landscape, as shown in the following screenshot:

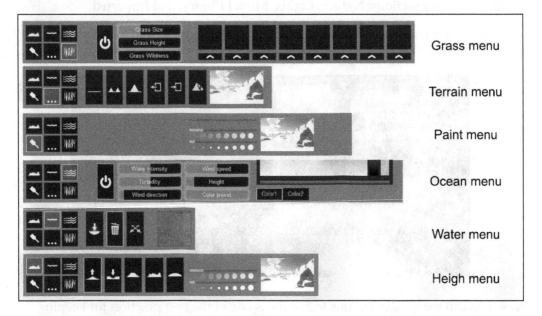

The **Water** and **Ocean** menus are very specific and you will probably only use these two features a couple of times. But what are the best practices for using the **Landscape** menu for exterior scenes?

Working with the Terrain tools

The landscape is composed of several elements, and Lumion provides the tools for each one. You may feel tempted to immediately sculpt the terrain using the tools available on the **Height** menu. However, a few aspects need to be taken into consideration in order to know which tools to use and when. Always think about what are you trying to accomplish and what the needs of the project are.

Are you creating a house in the forest with mountains? In that case, the **Terrain** menu has the better tools to produce those mountains. Are you creating an urban environment? The **Height** menu is the most suitable for that. Do you need to render a close-up of the building? In that case, the **Grass** and **Paint** menus may help most.

The best way to approach complex landscapes is by dividing them into sections and starting from the biggest section and moving to the smallest (where, usually, more detail is required).

Landscape types

Looking at the big picture, what stands out when it comes to the landscape you are trying to produce? There are different types of landscapes that include coast, valleys, mountains, plains, and hills. To produce these different landscape types, you will need to combine different tools and techniques. Let's consider the key points to produce some of these types.

Creating a coast using the Ocean and Terrain menus

To create a coast landscape, you need two elements: terrain and ocean. Working with them is not very difficult, and you only need to use two menus initially, as shown in the following screenshot:

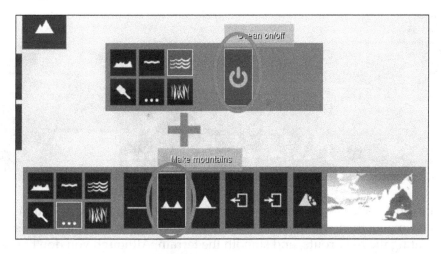

The process is very simple: on the **Terrain** menu, click on the **Make mountains** button, and then, on the **Ocean** menu, click on the **Ocean on/off** button. The **Ocean** menu is surprisingly simple to use and you can start by tweaking **Height** in case the ocean is too low or too high. After that, you will be more concerned with the artistic aspect and the mood and feeling you are trying to achieve. The **Color preset** setting gives you a handle to tweak the look of the water and then a combination of **Wave intensity** and **Turbidity** allows you to create something between a wild and paradisiacal ocean.

 If you need something quick and already set up for you, use the **Island preset** scene. From there, you can start sculpting the terrain with tools that you will see in the upcoming sections.

Suppose you think that the ocean looks great but are not interested in having mountains in your scene? Let's see which tools to use to sculpt the terrain into something more to your taste.

Creating a valley using the Water and Height menus

A valley is usually a low area between hills and, often, there is a river running through it. In this instance, you may want to leave the **Terrain** menu and have a look at the **Height** menu and the different tools available. Open the **Height** menu and you can see that there are four sculpting brushes available, as shown in the following screenshot:

In order to create a valley, you may want to use the **Make mountains** option under the **Terrain** menu; then, use the tools available in the **Height** menu to lower some areas, creating the river route, and smooth the terrain. Although you don't have to use the **Make mountains** to create a valley, the reality is that, with this option, you will not have to lower the terrain to create the hills.

 If your mountains are looking strange, press the *F7* key to show high-quality terrain in the viewport.

What about the river? The best option is to use the **Ocean** menu and then reduce the **Wave intensity** and **Turbidity** settings. The next step is to increase the **Wind speed** value and use **Wind direction** to make the water run parallel to the river channel.

It is still worth knowing that you can use the **Water** menu to add different types of water bodies to your scene, as shown in the following screenshot:

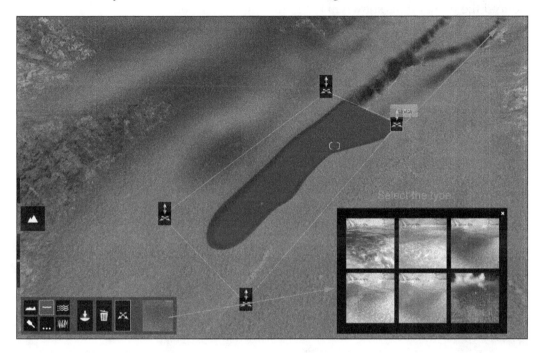

After selecting and placing the water body, you can use the **Up** and **Stretch** tools to tweak the size and height of the water body.

This may force you to choose between a river with an oceanic look and a river that is almost static with slight undulation. However, the **Water** menu may prove quite useful if you are looking for a pond or an icy look.

Creating a terrain using heightmaps

Eventually, you will come across a project where the terrain needs to be particularly detailed: for example, when you are reproducing a real location in an accurate way. Using the **Height** menu may not be practical at all, and you are forced to look for help on a terrain map. While working with the **Terrain** menu, it is possible you noticed the two buttons shown in the following screenshot:

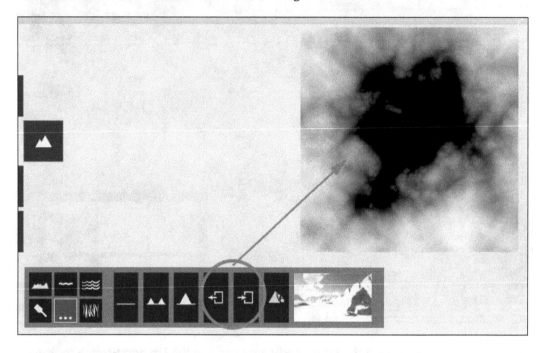

The way you are going to create the terrain or height map is defined first by the level of accuracy you need and next by whether you are trying to replicate a real-world location.

Guidelines to create heightmaps

To start creating this map, there are a few things you need to keep in mind. Firstly, Lumion has limits in terms of terrain, or in other words, the editable parts of the terrain in Lumion occupy a 2048 x 2048 m2 area. Even if you create a texture for a small area, Lumion will stretch the texture to the full extent of 2048 x 2048 meters.

Then, the height map is created by using a range of values between black and white. The colors indicate the following:

- **Black**: This is equal to a terrain height of 0 meters.
- **White**: This is equal to a terrain height of 200 meters.
- **Grayscale**: Each shade of gray is equal to 0.78 meters.

In case you need something higher than 200 meters, you can use 16 bit and even 32 bit images. When using an image of 16 bits, we will increase the height to 400 m, and when using one of 32 bits, we increase it to 600 m.

Tools used to create heightmaps

To create a heighmap manually, you need to use an image editor, such as Photoshop or GIMP. This will require time to create good results, but it gives the most flexibility possible, because using a brush you can literally sculpt the terrain. Since black is equal to 0 meters, it is a good start to fill the texture with the color black and then, using a brush with a low opacity, start to add the white color. Because you are using a brush with a low opacity, let's say 10 percent of opacity, each brush stroke is equal to roughly 20 meters of height.

In order to create a height map, we need to download some texture tools.

Download NVIDIA texture tools for Adobe Photoshop from the following URL:

```
https://developer.nvidia.com/nvidia-texture-
tools-adobe-photoshop
```

Download the GIMP DDS plugin from the following URL:

```
https://code.google.com/p/gimp-dds/
```

Obviously, you will need to check the result constantly in Lumion and see if you are getting the desired results. Lumion supports the following formats to load heightmaps:

- **BMP**: Windows bitmap
- **JPG**: Joint Photographic Experts Group
- **DDS**: DirectDraw Surface
- **PNG**: Portable Network Graphics

The final step is saving the heightmap as a 32 bit DDS in the 32F format using Nvidia's DDS plugin.

Another possibility is to use specialized 3D applications to create these maps. Creating and editing heightmaps may be practical when working with small-scale projects, but things start to get serious when you need high-quality heightmaps. Which 3D application can you use? Fortunately, there are some free and commercial applications that can help you:

- **L3DT (free/commercial)**: **Large 3D Terrain (L3DT)** is a Windows application for generating terrain maps and textures, and it is intended to help game developers and digital artists create vast high-quality 3D worlds. For more information, visit `http://www.bundysoft.com/L3DT/`.

- **World Machine (free edition/commercial)**: Powerful and flexible, World Machine combines procedural terrain creation, simulations of nature, and interactive editing to produce realistic-looking terrains quickly and easily. Go to `http://www.world-machine.com/` for more information on this.

- **Terragen (free edition/commercial)**: Terragen is very good at generating a ground texture and allows us to create and manipulate highly realistic terrains, both height field and procedural. For more information, visit `http://www.planetside.co.uk/`.

What if you want a specific real location? There are some places where you can get that information, and the following list provides some of them:

- US Geological Survey: `http://www.usgs.gov/`
- National Geospatial Intelligence Agency: `https://www.nga.mil/Pages/default.aspx`
- British Ordnance Survey: `http://www.ordnancesurvey.co.uk/`
- Landsat TM: `https://lta.cr.usgs.gov/TM`

There is another option that is simpler to use-Global Data Explorer. The **US Geological Survey (USGS)** is a scientific agency of the United States government, and they provide a useful application called Global Data Explorer, which can be used to locate real-world locations and export height maps.

 You can find Global Data Explorer via the following link:
`http://gdex.cr.usgs.gov/gdex/`.

After creating a free account, you can draw a rectangle selection and download the image, as shown in the following screenshot:

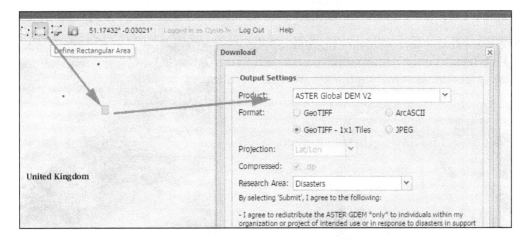

It is very important to set **Format** to **GeoTIFF - 1x1 Tiles**; otherwise, the images will be tiny or useless. Open the image in an image editor to perform some adjustments, as shown in the following screenshot:

You need to start by adjusting the levels because the image will be very dark and there will be small white dots (errors) in the image; these are not very difficult to fix.

There is another option you can use. Perhaps this is best solution for your project for the reason of being both accurate and at the same time doesn't require much work from your part.

Working with imported terrains

On some rare occasions, you may have a terrain provided by the Engineering team, for example Civil 3D. The other possibility is modeling it using an external 3D application.

You can use this terrain inside Lumion by exporting it as you would do with another 3D model. Once inside Lumion, you can assign the fantastic **Landscape** material to this 3D terrain, as shown in the following screenshot:

As you can see, this **Landscape** material is a fantastic way to easily blend the imported terrain with Lumion's terrain. This material goes even further because now it is as though the 3D model that you imported is part of the terrain, and this means that you can add grass and even paint textures on the 3D model imported. This is a great way to introduce two great features in Lumion.

Scattering elements with the Grass menu

An exterior scene, in most cases, would not be complete without some beautiful pasture. You can open the **Green Hills** scene under the **Examples** tab and see how the **Grass** menu can be used to create (a) neat-looking grass and (b) scattered plants and other elements present in a real pasture. The menu is very simple to use, as you can see in the following screenshot:

The three grass settings are used to control how the grass looks, but you can add some nifty elements using the thumbnails on the right-hand side. Click on the arrow and select the 3D model to be scattered. However, the grass will appear in the entire landscape, which can create some conflicts with the geometry of the floor. You may end up with grass inside your living room, but there is a quick way to solve that problem.

Choosing the landscape with the Paint menu

The **Paint** menu is where you can control how the landscape looks and what textures are used. You can change each texture individually, but it's always a good idea to change the landscape type first. As you can see in the following screenshot, there are 20 landscape types:

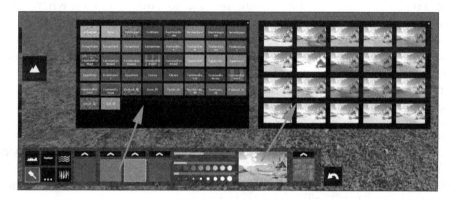

Also, you can mix textures from different landscapes. The great feature with this menu is that you can actually paint these textures wherever you want, and this can be used to remove grass from particular locations. The following annotated screenshot shows how easy the process is:

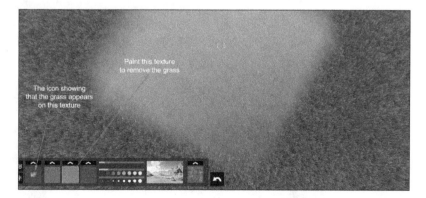

The first thumbnail shows an icon which indicates that grass will appear where this texture has been used. That means that you can use all the other three textures to paint and remove the grass from specific areas. This is particularly useful when you have a building that was placed on the terrain, and because grass is active, it will appear trespassing the 3D model. It is also useful if you want to create small paths and add more randomness to a garden where, for example, there is less grass around the tree's roots.

Summary

This chapter provided a solid foundation for producing exterior scenes. You learned how to successfully work with the **Landscape** menu. You also learned that working with complex scenes can be challenging but that this can be tackled by using the **Merge** scene functionality, which allows you to work with references in Lumion. You learned that the **Landscape** menu is not simply a menu where you can create an ocean or a river. It can be very powerful by using heightmaps along with four brushes, which let you sculpt the terrain to your needs. Further, you can also use external terrains and blend them neatly with Lumion's terrain, by using the **Landscape** material. Finally, you saw how to use the **Grass** menu to create a complex lawn and how to use the **Paint** menu not only to control the grass in the landscape but also to tweak the look of your terrain.

In the next chapter, you will learn some techniques to create materials that have a big impact on the level of realism. We will have a closer look at Lumion's physically based materials and several ways that you can use materials in Lumion. After that, you will learn how to clean and create your own seamless textures and other maps essential to creating believable materials in Lumion.

5
Working with Physically Based Materials

Physically based rendering materials will probably sound like something really technical and out-of-the-scope for you. However, if you look at the 3D model as a skeleton, the materials bring life to your scene. Not only is it necessary in terms of aesthetics, but you can play with colors and contrast as a composition tool to convey the message for a specific project as well. Working with materials is not a simple task of assigning a material to a particular surface; you have to learn how to bend them to your will.

In this chapter, you are going to learn what physically based materials are, where they are in Lumion and how to work with them. As a plus, you will learn some techniques to create your own textures to use in Lumion. To give you a heads up, have a look at the following list of topics that we are going to cover:

- A quick overview of Lumion's materials
- What is a physically based material?
- Three options for materials in Lumion
- Normal maps – how to create them
- Glowing materials
- How to improve reflections
- Using movies as textures
- Using the **Standard** material
- Making your own materials
- Making seamless textures

As you can see, we will be covering a lot of subjects and technical aspects that will significantly improve the method you use to work with materials, and this is the best way to take full advantage of what Lumion has to offer.

Materials, and why they are essential

In the 3D world, materials and textures are nearly as important as the 3D geometry that composes the scene. A material defines the optical properties of an object when hit by a ray of light. In other words, a material defines how the light interacts with the surface, and textures can help not only to control the color (diffuse), but also the reflections and glossiness.

It's not difficult to understand that textures are another essential part of a good material, and if your goal is to achieve believable results, you need textures or images of real elements like stone, wood, brick, and other natural elements. Textures can bring detail to your surface that otherwise would require geometry to look good.

In that case, how can Lumion help you and, most importantly, what are the best practices to work with materials? Let's have a look at the next section which will provide the answer.

A quick overview of Lumion's materials

Lumion always had a good library of materials to assign to your 3D model, and in *Chapter 3, Creating an Interior Scene with Lumion*, you learned that Lumion introduced the Physically-based rendering materials in more recent versions. Although we touched upon this subject in *Chapter 3, Creating an Interior Scene with Lumion*, we are going to have a better look at what **Physically-Based Rendering (PBR)** materials really mean for us as artists.

The reality is that PBR is more of a concept than a set of rules, and each render engine will implement slightly differently. The good news for us as users is that these materials follow realistic shading and lighting systems to accurately represent real-world materials.

You can find excellent information regarding PBR on the following sites:

- http://www.marmoset.co/toolbag/learn/pbr-theory
- http://www.marmoset.co/toolbag/learn/pbr-practice
- https://www.allegorithmic.com/pbr-guide

More than 600 materials are already prepared to be assigned directly to your 3D model and, by default, they should provide a realistic and appropriate material. The Lumion team has also made an effort to create a better and simpler interface, as you can see in the following screenshot:

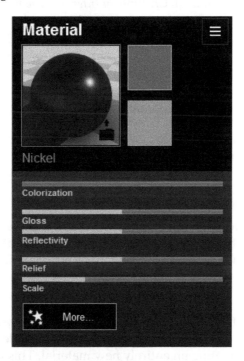

The interface was simplified, showing only the most common and essential settings. If you need more control over the material, click on the **More...** button to have access to extra functionalities. One word of caution: the material preview, which in this case is the sphere, will not reflect the changes you perform using the settings available. For example, if you change the main texture, the sphere will continue to show the previous material.

A good practice to tweak materials is to assign the material to the surface, use the viewport to check how the settings are affecting the material, and then do a quick render. The viewport will try to show the final result, but there's nothing like a quick render to see how the material really looks when Lumion does all the lighting and shading calculations.

Working with materials in Lumion – three options

You probably noticed in *Chapter 3, Creating an InteriorScene with Lumion*, we mentioned that there are three options to work with materials in Lumion:

- Using Lumion's materials
- Using the imported materials that you can create on your favorite modeling application
- Creating materials using Lumion's Standard material

Let's have a look at each one of these options and see how they can help you and when they best suit your project.

Using Lumion's materials

The first option is obvious; you are using Lumion and it makes sense using Lumion's materials, but you may feel constrained by what is available at Lumion's material library. However, instead of thinking, "I only have 600 materials and I cannot find what I need!", you need to look at the materials library also as a template to create other materials.

For example, if none of the brick materials is similar to what you need, nothing stops you from using a brick material, changing the **Gloss** and **Reflection** values, and loading a new texture, creating an entirely new material. This is made possible by using the **Choose Color Map** button, as shown in the following screenshot:

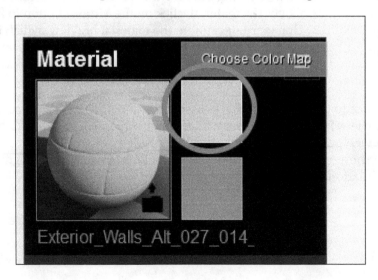

When you click on the **Choose Color Map** button, a new window appears where you can navigate to the folder where the texture is saved. What about the second square? The one with a purple color? Let's see the answer in the next section.

Normal maps and their functionality

The purple square you just saw is where you can load the normal map. And what is a normal map? Firstly, a normal map is not a **bump** map. A bump map uses a color range from black to white and in some ways is more limited than a normal map. The following screenshots show the clear difference between these two maps:

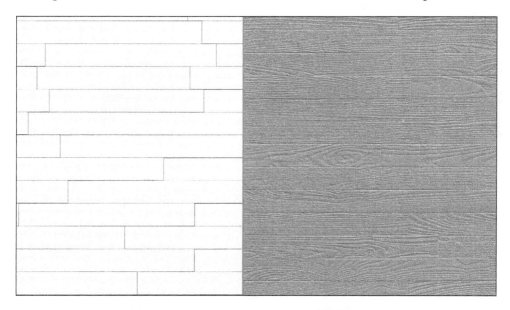

The map on the left is a bump map and you can see that the level of detail is not the same that we can get with a normal map. A normal map consists of red, green, and blue colors that represent the x, y, and z coordinates. This allows a 2D image to represent depth and Lumion uses this depth information to fake lighting details based on the color associated with the 3D coordinate.

The perks of using a normal map

Why should you use normal maps? Keep in mind that Lumion is a real-time rendering engine and, as you saw previously, there is the need to keep a balance between detail and geometry. If you add too much detail, the 3D model will look gorgeous but Lumion's performance will suffer drastically. On the other hand, you can have a low-poly 3D model and fake detail with a normal map.

Using a normal map for each material has a massive impact on the final quality you can get with Lumion. Since these maps are so important, how can you create one?

Tips to create normal maps

As you will understand, we cannot cover all the different techniques to create normal maps. However, you may find something to suit your workflow in the following list:

- **Photoshop using an action script called nDo**: Teddy Bergsman is the author of this fantastic script. It is a free script that creates a very accurate normal map of any texture you load in Photoshop in seconds.

> To download and see how to install this script, visit the following link:
> `http://www.philipk.net/ndo.html`
> Here you can find a more detailed tutorial on how to use this nDo script:
> `http://www.philipk.net/tutorials/ndo/ndo.html`

This script has three options to create normal maps. The default option is **Smooth**, which gives you a blurry normal map. Then you have the **Chisel Hard** option to generate a very sharp and subtle normal map but you don't have much control over the final result. The **Chisel Soft** option is similar to the **Chisel Hard** except that you have full control over the intensity and bevel radius. This script also allows you to sculpt and combine several normal maps.

- **Using the Quixel NDO application**: From the same creator, we have a more capable and optimized application called **Quixel NDO**. With this application, you can sculpt normal maps in real-time, build your own normal maps without using textures, and preview everything with the 3DO material preview. This is quite useful because you don't have to save the normal map and see how it looks in Lumion. 3DO (which comes free with NDO) has a physically based renderer and lets you load a 3D model to see how the texture looks.

> Find more information including a free trial here:
> `http://quixel.se/dev/ndo`

- **GIMP with the normalmap plugin**: If you want to use free software, a good alternative is GIMP. There is a great plugin called **normalmap**, which does good work not only by creating a normal map but also by providing a preview window to see the tweaks you are making.

> To download this plugin, visit the following link:
> `https://code.google.com/p/gimp-normalmap/`

- **Do it online with NormalMap-Online**. In case you don't want to install another application, the best option is doing it online. In that case, you may want to have a look at **NormalMap-Online**, as shown in the following screenshot:

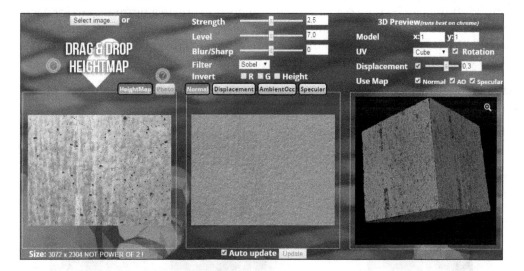

- The process is extremely simple as you can see from the preceding screenshot. You load the image and automatically get a normal map, and on the right-hand side there is a preview to show how the normal map and the texture work together. Christian Petry is the man behind this tool that will help to create sharp and accurate normal maps. He is a great guy and if you like this online application, please consider supporting an application that will save you time and money.

[Find this online tool here:
http://cpetry.github.io/NormalMap-Online/]

- Don't forget to use a good combination of **Strength** and **Blur/Sharp** to create a well-balanced map. You need the correct amount of detail; otherwise your normal map will be too noisy in terms of detail.

However, Lumion being a user-friendly application, gives you a hand on this topic by providing a tool to create a normal map automatically from a texture you import.

Creating a normal map with Lumion's relief feature

By now, creating a normal map from a texture is not something too technical or even complex, but it can be time consuming if you need to create a normal map for each texture. This is a wise move because it will remove the need for extra detail for the model to look good. With this in mind, Lumion's team created a new feature that allows you to create a normal map for any texture you import.

After loading the new texture, the next step is to click on the **Create Normal Map** button, as highlighted in the following screenshot:

Lumion then creates a normal map based on the texture imported, and you have the ability to invert the map by clicking on the **Flip Normal Map direction** button, as highlighted in the preceding screenshot.

Once Lumion creates the normal map, you need a way to control how the normal map affects the material and the light. For that, you need to use the **Relief** slider, as shown in the following screenshot:

Using this slider is very intuitive; you only need to move the slider and see the adjustments on the viewport, since the material preview will not be updated. The previous screenshot is a good example of that, because even when we loaded a wood texture, the preview still shows a concrete material.

Again, this means you can easily use the settings from one material and use that as a base to create something completely new. But how good is the normal map that Lumion creates for you? Have a look for yourself in the following screenshot:

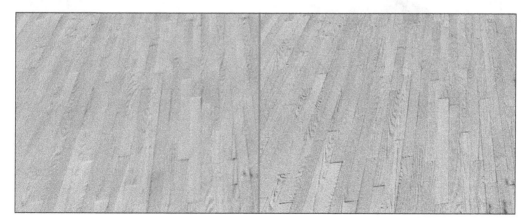

On the left hand side, we have a wood floor material with a normal map that Lumion created. The right-hand side image is the same material but the normal map was created using the free nDo script for Photoshop. There is a big difference between the image on the left and the image on the right, and that is related to the normal maps used in this case. You can see clearly that the normal map used for the image on the right achieves the goal of bringing more detail to the surface. The difference is that the normal map that Lumion creates in some situations is too blurry, and for that reason we end up losing detail.

Before we explore a few more things regarding creating custom materials in Lumion, let's have a look at another useful feature in Lumion.

Glowing materials and the Emissive setting

Are glowing materials useful? The answer is: yes, in particular situations. In the end, it is attention to detail that contributes to creating a believable image. There are several situations where glowing materials provide the right touch to creating a believable scene. For example, in a scene where light bulbs are glowing, with respect to the particular light spots, adding glowing helps to sell the image as real. Another good example is shown in the following screenshot:

It looks great with the fire but there is something missing in this image: the light and glow produced by the fire and the wood burning.

One simple way to solve this issue is by creating a small geometry such as a cube or a tube, importing that geometry into the scene, and placing it in the fireplace. After assigning a wood material to the imported geometry, you need to tweak the **Colorization** slider and for this particular situation, select a red-orange color, as shown in the following screenshot:

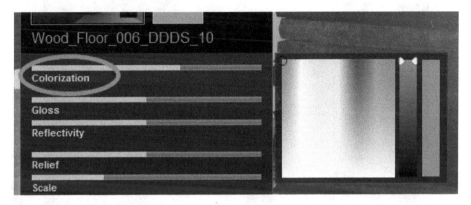

This will change the overall color of the object but will not create any glow. To create the glow effect, you need to follow the steps shown in the following screenshot:

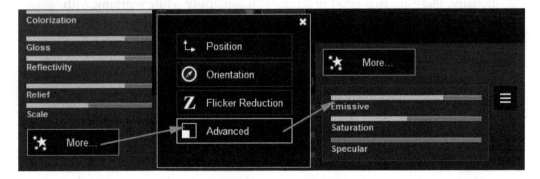

Click on the **More** settings button and select the **Advanced** category, which in turn gives you access to the **Emissive** slider. The amount of **Emissive** will depend on your scene, the mood you are trying to achieve, and the lighting present. But as you can see in the following screenshot, a simple technique like this can make a big difference:

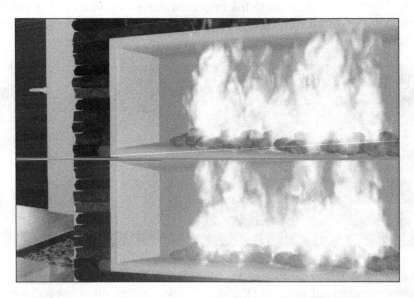

Additionally, there are two good practices you can apply while working with materials that will help bring life to your scene. Let's start with the first, which involves how the materials reflect light.

Improving material reflections

We have already mentioned the fact that Lumion, in order to provide real-time feedback on materials, light, and shadows needs to use some shortcuts that have some impact on the final quality.

Calculating reflections and glossiness is something that can take a big toll in terms of performance. However, Lumion gives you the opportunity to improve those reflections in all materials, in particular with glass objects. Let's have a look at the following render made with Lumion:

Have a closer look at the windows and see how the reflections don't look that great. They even reflect a horizon that is not visible at all (because we have other houses in the background). This is not the end of the world because you can solve these using two features in Lumion. You can use the **Reflection** effect with the **Photo mode** or **Movie mode**, but that option will be covered later in this book. For now, use the **Reflection Control** ball which you can find on the **Lights And Utilities Library** option, as shown in the following screenshot:

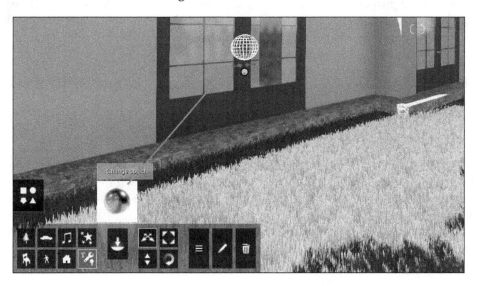

One key aspect for this technique to work is where you are going to place this **Reflection Control** ball. There isn't any specific set of rules for this; it's more like trial and error in order to find a good place that provides good reflections. In the previous screenshot, we need to put the reflection ball higher in order to achieve something like this:

Now we have a proper reflection on the glass and although this situation isn't very noticeable, the reflections on the materials are improved, delivering a natural look. Keep this technique in mind when doing an animation because it will provide balanced quality and, at the same time, not increase the render time.

Next, you will learn a simple technique to add a special touch to your 3D scene, by using a video as a texture.

Using a video as a texture

This is a particularly useful technique for TV and other screens that will look much better if you play a video. It is a simple thing but it helps to sell the scene as real, and the workflow is very simple. You only need to apply a **Standard** material and click on the **Choose Color Map** button to load a texture, but instead, select a video that is under 50MB in size. After selecting and importing the video as a texture, the icon changes to a filmstrip indicating that you have now a video, as shown in the following screenshot:

The video will start to play on loop, which means you need to take that into consideration when creating an animation. You will find out that something so simple can actually make a huge difference in the final output, be it a still image or an animation.

However, sometimes Lumion's materials are not enough and you need something more specific. We already saw several options to create normal maps but there are more aspects involved in creating materials to be used in Lumion.

Custom materials for Lumion

As already mentioned, we have at least three options to have materials in Lumion. The first option is the one we just saw: using Lumion's materials. In most cases, the materials available will be enough for your project, but there are always special requests from the client to use a particular material and that leads us to the second and third options.

Creating materials with an external 3D application

The second option is to use the imported materials that you create in your favorite modeling application. This makes a lot of sense, because if you are modeling, it's always a good idea to do the following:

- Do a quick render to check how the geometry is looking and whether there is a need for more work in certain areas. It also helps to see where you can have better highlights.

- Assign a texture to the surface and see how the model and the texture combine and if there is a need for minor adjustments.

Then you can easily export everything using FBX or COLLADA, because once the 3D model is imported, Lumion recognizes the texture.

 If you export UVs along with the geometry, don't forget to set the **Scale** slider to **0** in order for Lumion to use the imported texture coordinates instead of automatically applying the texture coordinates.

You really don't have to do anything else unless there are some reflective materials. Don't forget to use the default material node available in the 3D application, and don't use the materials from V-Ray, Mental Ray, or Corona. Also, there is no point in using a texture to control reflection and glossiness, since Lumion will only recognize the diffuse texture.

 If you are wondering what a diffuse texture is, a diffuse texture, in simple words, is the image file with color information that will transform a surface into a wood floor or a brick wall.

What is the third option? The third option is to create materials inside Lumion. Is there a big difference between these two last options? The difference between each option is the technique used. The second option involves a good knowledge of the 3D application you are using to create UVs or something like **box mapping** to place the textures in the correct location. The third option is slightly easier to use because most of the time Lumion does a good job applying the texture.

Although creating the materials using an external 3D application is one good way to create a material, the truth is that you end up having more options by creating materials inside Lumion. For that, you need to use the **Standard** material.

Lumion's Standard material

The **Standard** material can sometimes be overlooked as just a quick way to import and use textures. The interface of this material is not something new because we already used it several times during this book. So, why the need to talk about it again?

There are some important features that you need to take into consideration while working with this material:

- **Controlling glossiness with the normal map**: This is not something new because in *Chapter 3, Creating an Interior Scene with Lumion*, you learned how to control reflections with the alpha channel. In this case, you apply the same principle but instead of saving the alpha channel on the diffuse texture, you save the alpha channel of the normal map.

- Reduction flickering with the **Flicker Reduction** slider: Only use this slider if you are too lazy to correct overlapping surfaces, which means making sure that the surfaces are offset a small amount in your 3D application.

- Using the **Texture Alpha** option: You can use this option for either of two purposes. They are:

  - **Color Map Alpha Masks Reflectivity**: This means that the alpha channel in your **Color Map** is used as a Reflectivity mask.

  - **Color Map Alpha Clips Object**: This is a great utility to cut out complex geometry without too much effort. For that, you need to create a texture that is white for transparent areas and black for fully opaque sections. You can get an idea of how it works by having a look at the following screenshot that shows on the left the Alpha map used to create the grid shown on the right hand side:

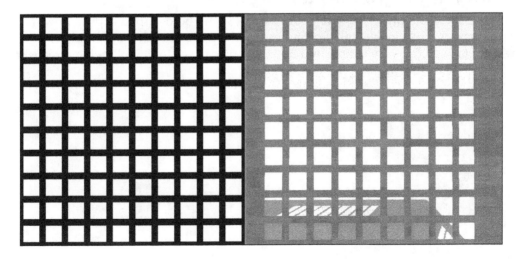

The **Standard** material can seem intimidating but, after this brief explanation, you not only see how it works, and what is possible to do but the way for you to learn would be to try it yourself. Create some simple scenes like a cube and test all of the features mentioned in this chapter.

But even with the **Standard** material, you need textures to use and apply to the 3D geometry. The following sections are going to help you find diffuse maps and create your own reflection and glossiness maps.

Finding textures and eliminating highlights

There are some places on the Internet where we can find good images that can be used, and maybe here we can find what we need. They are:

- Flickr
- Stock.xchg
- iStockphoto
- deviantART
- Textures.com

Another option is to pick up your camera and start creating your own library with various textures. However, it doesn't matter if you download the textures or use your own images, you will always face the problem of uneven lighting and highlights. That is not the end of the world because there are some techniques to create textures with an even lighting.

Fixing highlights on textures

For the sake of simplicity, we are going to stick with Photoshop to explain how the process works. Obviously, the techniques can be applied to other applications so we will try to keep this very simple and basic, as you can see in the following screenshot:

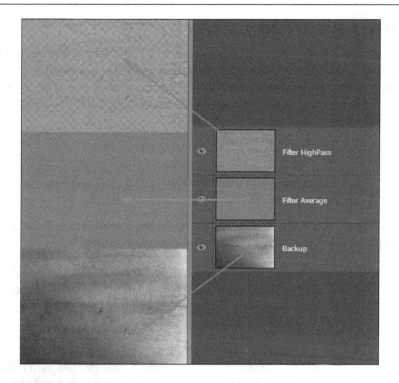

You need to follow these steps:

1. Create a copy of the image.

2. Select the first layer (the one on the bottom) and apply the **Average** filter found under the **Blur** menu. This filter takes the average of the colors in the photo and fills a layer with that color, a uniform color.

3. Select the second layer and set the **Blending** mode to **Linear Light** and the **Opacity** to **50** percent.

4. Next, select the **HighPass** filter and play with the radius (the values will depend on the size and resolution of the texture). Adjust the radius until you get a uniform light on the texture, that is, no dark or bright areas.

However, after this there is something else you need to do in order to use these textures in Lumion, making it seamless.

Creating seamless textures

A seamless texture is nothing out of this world. In simple terms, a seamless texture is an image that can be placed side-by-side with itself without creating a noticeable seam between the two copies. They are not that difficult to create. The trick is making them less repetitive so that when you apply them on a big area, there isn't any noticeable pattern.

 If you don't want to lose time with this, Cgtextures.com is a good place to go because they provide tiled or seamless textures.

Again, we will have to stick with Photoshop to create a seamless texture, since we cannot cover here all of the image editor applications available.

 If you are not too concerned about getting perfect textures, you may want to have a look at the free seamless textures generator available at: http://www.the-orange-box.com/.

Start by creating a square texture and keep in mind the image size. After that, select the **Offset** tool and, in both the **Horizontal** and **Vertical** text box, insert the image size divided by two, as shown in the following screenshot:

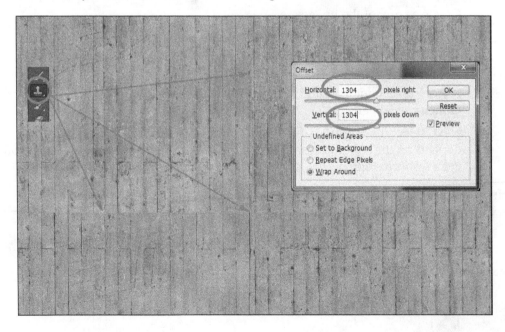

In the preceding screenshot, the image was a square of 2608 by 2608px, so we used a value of 1304px. Your image, like the one shown in the preceding screenshot, will have some seams that need to be corrected. The only way to do that is by manually using the **Clone** tool to clone pixel information from one point to another until the seam disappears.

If you want to take this texture to the next level repeat all the processes again until, no matter how many times you offset, the texture will not have any visible seam.

Creating reflection and glossiness maps

Creating a reflection and a glossiness map is not that difficult, but please keep in mind that these are just some generic steps to create these kinds of textures. You always need to tweak the textures by loading them into Lumion and seeing if the result is what you like.

Starting with the reflection map, duplicate the diffuse texture and desaturate by pressing the *Shift + Ctrl + U* key combination. Using the levels exaggerates the contrast in the dark range, but keep in mind that a reflection map controls where the reflection happens and how strong it is. So, a value close to black will not reflect at all, while a white area will be fully reflective.

The same principle applies to the glossiness map, but in this case remember that the glossiness map controls how sharp or blurry the reflection is. In the end, you may end up with something similar to what you can see in the following screenshot:

Another way to create textures to use in Lumion is by using the Bitmap2Material, which allows you to generate all those PBR outputs from a single input image. Have a look here:

https://www.allegorithmic.com/products/bitmap2material

Summary

Physically based rendering materials aren't that scary, would you agree? In reality, Lumion makes this feature almost unnoticeable by making it so simple. You learned what this feature involves and how you can take full advantage of materials that make your render more believable. You learned the importance of using normal maps and how to create them using a variety of tools for all flavors. You also saw how we can easily improve material reflections without compromising the speed and quality of the render.

You also learned another key aspect of Lumion: flexibility to create your own materials using the **Standard** material. The **Standard** material, although slightly different from the other materials available in Lumion, lets you play with the reflections, glossiness, and other settings that are essential. On top of all of this, you learned how to create textures.

In the next chapter, you will learn how to bring life to your video by using different animation techniques. This includes not only how to use Lumion's effects to control animations, but also how planning and storyboards can help achieve a higher quality.

6
Animation Techniques in Lumion

The true power of Lumion lies in its ability to produce videos easily. You may notice that there aren't any tools in the **Build** mode to create animations, even when you place some 3D animated models on your scene. All the magic happens inside the **Movie** mode, where you can find the tools to bring your scene to life.

However, in spite of all the aid Lumion provides to create animations, you still need to learn the best practices for creating animations inside Lumion and importing your own animations. With this in mind, the following list of topics will be covered in this chapter:

- Planning your scene
- Tips to export animations
- Using a storyboard
- A quick overview of Lumion's **Movie** mode
- How to import and control animations
- The **Move** effect
- The **Advanced move** effect
- The **Mass move** effect

With all of these topics in mind, let's start with the most important stage before animation, which is planning.

Planning your scene

You probably noticed that, over and over, the subject of planning is brought up before we start any actual work. The reason is that planning is the most important stage before you start actually doing anything.

The same is true when working with animations and there are a few important aspects that need your consideration in order for you to easily create a video.

Tips to export animations

Starting with animations you import, you need to keep in mind the following list when planning and creating animations using Maya, Blender, or any other 3D software:

- It is only possible to import animations made with the move, scale, and rotate parameters. This means that is not possible to import Vertex, Morph, or Bone animations in Lumion.

- When creating an animation, you need to set your frame rate to 25 frames per second or PAL.

- Export the object with the animation using the FBX file format.

- You can export the animation with the COLLADA file format, but the interpolation between the key frames will be linear.

Keeping these guidelines in mind will help create animations that can be used in Lumion and helps to avoid some issues, such as converting an animation from 30fps to 25fps. However, what about creating animations in Lumion? What points would be good to keep in mind?

Using a simple storyboard

What is a **storyboard**? It is a graphic representation of the camera path through the scene. A storyboard for a small project doesn't need to be something very complex. But what is the point of using a storyboard? In the beginning, it may sound like an extra step but, in reality, the storyboard can help you with the following:

- **Being on the same page with your client**: It is really easy to create misconceptions and after all the hard work, the client may simply say: "This is not what I had in mind". On the other hand, it can help to share the vision you have for the video.

- **Saving time and money**: With a storyboard, you can plan what you need, when you need, and how things will be laid out.

Although a storyboard can be something very simple, the truth is that the more information you, add the easier it will be while creating the animation. You can add things like where the cameras will be, what you will be filming, how the elements are composed within the frame, and in some situations, you can even define the mood and colors to be used. Consider how something that will perhaps take a couple of hours can save you days of trial and error.

This chapter is dedicated to animations in Lumion and not to camera animation. That is something we will cover later in this book. For now, let's see where we can create these animations.

A quick overview of Lumion's Movie mode

With your experience using Lumion, knowing where the **Movie** mode is located certainly is not a difficult task. In Lumion, a movie or video is divided into smaller sections called **clips**. The following screenshot gives you a good idea of how to create a clip in Lumion:

The clips you create are the base for the animations you are filming, and you will notice this when creating and tweaking the animations. Of course, it is possible to change the clip's length but it is always a good idea to have the length established from the beginning.

What effects are needed in order to create animations in Lumion? In the **Movie** effect library there is a tab called **Objects**, where you can find these effects.

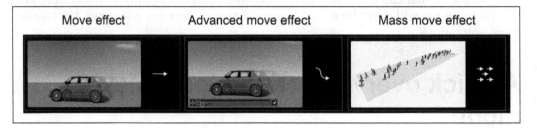

We are going to cover all three of these effects in this chapter but before we jump to that section, let's see how to import animations in Lumion and control them using clips.

How to import animations

An animation is attached to the 3D model that you export. Let's consider that you want to animate a car going from point A to point B in 30 seconds. Keeping in mind what you learned in the section *Tips to export animations*, you exported the 3D model using an FBX file format. So far so good, but now you need to import that into Lumion. How? The same way you import another 3D model, with the difference that you need to tick the **Import animations** box (as shown in the following screenshot) so that Lumion imports the animation.

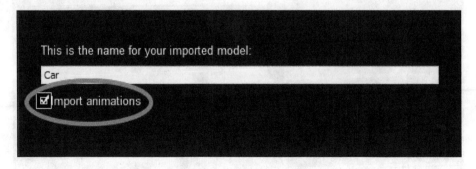

Nonetheless, after placing the 3D model you can see that the model keeps moving in a loop, which can be annoying when you have multiple imported animations. In the **Build** mode, there is nothing you can do to stop this loop from happening, but you can place all the imported animations inside a layer and then hide that layer. But how can you control an imported animation if they keep playing in a loop?

Controlling imported animations

As mentioned, there is nothing we can do while working in **Build** mode, but don't panic because it is possible to control or at least use an imported animation.

 A word of caution: the process, although not complex, involves good planning and use of layers to hide and show animations.

In order to work with imported animations, there is one essential question you need to answer: how long is the animation?

This is information you really need. Why? Let's say the imported animation is in total 8 seconds or 200 frames. It is imperative that the clip you create is only 8 seconds long. Why? Because if the clip isn't 8 seconds long and the object is still on frame, you will see the 3D model going back to the original position and repeating the same animation.

Simple animations with the Move effect

The video you produce depends on what the client wants but, usually, the movie you create will be something simple with some tracking shots of a few seconds.

 It will make your life easier if you create short clips instead of having massive clips. It's a more flexible approach and makes editing the movie a lot easier.

What are a few things you need to animate? People walking or swimming and definitely some cars moving around. When you need to animate a 3D model going from point A to point B in a straight line, the best tool to use is the **Move** effect. How does it work and what is the best way to use this effect? The principle behind the **Move** effect is very simple, as you can see from the following screenshot:

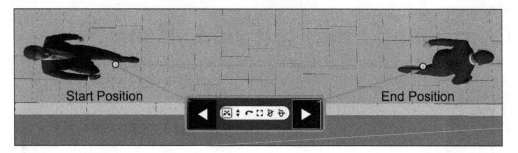

After adding this effect to the clip in question, you need to specify where the start and end positions are. However, there are a few things to keep in mind:

- You have to use the **Move** effect to animate all the objects in the scene. There isn't any option to apply the **Move** effect to individual 3D models.

- When defining a new path for another 3D model, don't forget to always press the **Start Position** button first. This will help to keep consistency during the workflow and will help to understand in which location all the 3D models start their path.

- If the path is too short, once the 3D model reaches the end of it, it will turn back and start walking. Play the animation more than once to make sure the path is long enough.

- Do a render with a low resolution. You will always find mistakes even after checking everything on the viewport.

As you can see, the **Move** effect is great and perfect for simple animations. However, if you need to animate a person walking around the corner, the **Move** effect is not suitable. You need the **Advanced move** effect.

Curved paths with the Advanced move effect

Don't let the name of this effect deceive you. The difference between the **Move** effect and the **Advanced move** effect is that, with the latter, you can use keyframes to create more complex animations, as shown in the following screenshot:

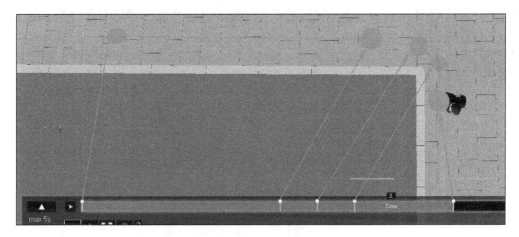

Although the effect seems great, what is the best way to use it? Have a look at the following list:

- Start by creating a keyframe for the initial position, move the time bar to the end and create another keyframe by simply moving the 3D model to the desired position.
- The time bar represents the length of your clip, so use this to avoid creating an animation that ends in a loop.
- Add a third keyframe where you want the 3D model to change direction.
- As shown in the previous screenshot, keep adding additional keyframes to create a smooth turn.
- Use the **Time** offset if you want to delay the animation in relation to the clip. This is a great way to avoid that look when the animation starts exactly with the clip. A few seconds of delay creates a good transition and doesn't look fake.

When working with small scenes, these two effects will help create a scene full of life and that doesn't involve much work, since the number of 3D models you have to animate are few. But what about an urban scene with loads of people and cars moving around? Do you have to animate individual 3D models using the **Move** or **Advanced move** effects? The answer is no and let's see why.

Making good use of the Mass move effect

You certainly are making good use of the **Mass placement** tool, which allows you to place a great variety of 3D models and bring randomness and uniqueness to the scene. But when it's time to animate all of these 3D models, the **Move** and **Advanced move** effects are not the best options. Instead, you need to use the **Mass move** effect and, as shown in the following screenshot, it's not that difficult to utilize:

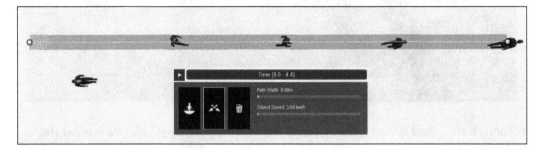

Placing the path is the first step you need to perform and you are not constrained to a single path. The path you create sets two important aspects: the length of the animation and its direction. But there is one essential point that you need to keep in mind in order for this effect to work, which is that the 3D models need to be on top of the path (the gray strip you see on the screen). For example, in the previous screenshot, one of the men was left out of the path and, for that reason, when you play the animation he will stay in the same position.

One way you can solve this is by moving the 3D model on top of the path or increasing the **Path Width** value in order to cover the location where the 3D model is. Another thing that you don't need to worry about is that the path will only work with objects that are animated, such as people walking and cars moving. This means that if there is a tree on top of the path, the tree will remain static when you play the animation.

And finally, don't forget that cars and people move at different speeds, which you can tweak by changing the **Object Speed** setting.

Summary

Although this was a small chapter, the workflow you learned here is an important step to create professional and efficient animations. In this chapter, your focus was on how to create animations using imported 3D models or some of the native Lumion models.

However, you also learned that planning is at the heart of every successful animation and that this planning can be achieved by using a simple storyboard to set up scenes and camera movements. Then, you saw how to efficiently import animations and control them using a simple clip. After this, you learned how to use three simple but efficient effects to create animations that can bring life and uniqueness to your scenes.

Nevertheless, these effects are just the start. There is so much you can do with effects and that is something we will cover in the next chapter. Also, we will start to produce still images with the help of the **Photo** mode and add a special touch with effects.

7
Producing a Still Image with Lumion

Throughout this book, you have been working really hard to build a well-optimized scene. This has involved importing a 3D model, assigning materials, and then adding more content using Lumion's library. However, now that you have a scene how can you export it? How can you show the world what you have been working on? There are several ways you can do this, but in this specific chapter you will learn the best techniques to create still images using the **Photo** mode. This is perhaps the most requested medium to present the information the client requires. The following list shows some of the topics we are going to cover:

- Quick overview: **Photo** mode
- Saving and loading camera positions
- **Built** mode with effects
- Saving and loading effects
- Adding effects
- Photo and movie effects
- Sun study–a useful tool
- Shadow effect to correct shadows
- Realistic reflections with the Reflection effect
- Two-point perspective effect
- Improving illumination with Global Illumination and Hyperlight®

One thing that is worth mentioning is that you will benefit a lot from having a quick look at the next chapter. The truth is that creating still images and animations are very close subjects in nature, and in Lumion what you need in order to create a still image is very similar to what you need to create an animation. Actually, if your primary goal is to create animations and then some still images, you can do everything in the **Movie** mode.

With the next chapter, something that it is worth learning is how to create a good composition. Yes, just because you have a camera, even virtual, doesn't automatically make you a good photographer.

And before we start with the *Quick overview* section, you need to keep in mind that the effects you will learn here can also be applied in the **Movie** mode.

A quick overview–the Photo mode

The **Photo** mode is where you can find all the tools needed if you are only interested in creating still images. Let's have a quick look at the interface for this mode and explore some useful features:

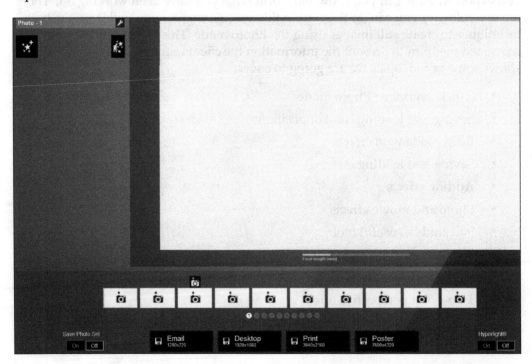

This interface may look different if you are using a version previous to Lumion 5 but, overall, the most important features you need to produce a still image are the same. What are the best practices in order to take full advantage of this menu?

Saving and loading camera positions

This is one of the most important features you need to keep in mind to create stunning images. You can access this feature in the **Photo** mode by using the bottom section, as shown in the following screenshot:

However, during the process of creating a 3D world, you eventually came across really good camera positions. It's true that you can jump to the **Photo** mode and save the camera position but a more efficient way is by using the following keyboard shortcuts:

- *CTRL + 0, 1, 2 to 9*: This shortcut is used to save up to 10 camera positions that are stored in **Photo Set 1**
- *SHIFT + 0, 1, 2 to 9*: This shortcut is used to load saved camera positions that you can find stored in **Photo Set 1**

This will certainly increase your workflow's speed but there is another feature that is worth mentioning and using.

The Build mode with effects

Using effects is a great way to enhance the scene, but sometimes it may be difficult to tweak certain areas. The viewport in **Photo** mode is not that big so one good practice is using the **Build with effects** button, as shown in the following screenshot:

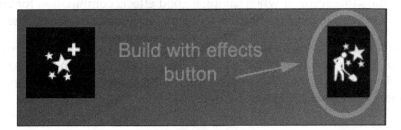

This makes it possible for you to get back to the **Build** mode but all the effects will become active and you can see them in action, like for example when working with the **Rain** or **Snow** effects. Using this mode gives you the opportunity to see if the effect is doing a good job, in particular, when you have to tweak shadows and the depth of field. One word of caution: too many effects will make the viewport very slow, such as if you have the Global Illumination effect applied. It is always a good idea to test just a few effects at a time.

Another feature that is very useful is the ability to save and load stacks of effects in different projects. Let's have a look at it.

Saving and loading effects

While you are working with **Photo** mode, you may use the same effects over and over in multiple projects and in the end, the settings will not differ that much. Lumion lets you save a stack of effects as a Lumion movie effects file (*lme) that can be loaded into a different project. The process is extremely simple, as shown in the following screenshot:

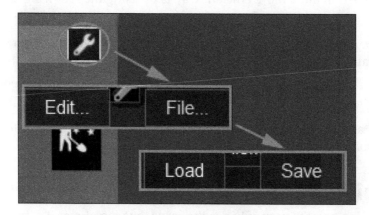

Under the **File** menu, you can find two submenus that let you **Save** or **Load** a Lumion movie effects file. This can prove to be practical when trying different settings for the same scene or when saving a good effects combination for later use. It is a simple technique but the ability to create presets of effects is priceless.

Next, we will start covering some effects that can be used to improve the quality of your image. However, before we start, there is something you need to know regarding the effects mentioned in this chapter: there aren't any magical settings that will automatically create a fantastic render.

A beginner often thinks that there is a secret formula to create beautiful art and tends to forget that experience, hard work, and practice is what makes a good piece of art. The following effects are just a small selection of what is available, but they truly can make all the difference in your project.

Photo and movie effects

As mentioned at the beginning of this chapter, most of the effects can be applied in either **Photo** or **Movie** mode. For that reason, the knowledge you acquire here can and should be used when creating animations.

For the next effects, we will firstly begin by explaining why the effect is useful, and secondly offer some tips to use it.

Sun Study – a useful tool

The first effect you can use is the Sun Study and this effect lets you pinpoint a geographical location of your project. This affects the sun and the shadows produced which in turn lets the architect see how these two elements affect the building and the surroundings.

This effect can be found under the **World** tab and allows a very accurate selection of the building's location by using the latitude and longitude values.

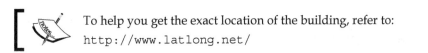

To help you get the exact location of the building, refer to: http://www.latlong.net/

Shadow effect to correct shadows

Shadows are essential to create a believable render but, at the same time, they are very expensive to calculate and simulate. To avoid any flickering and shadow artifacts, Lumion applies the shadow on top of every surface with a small offset. This small offset sometimes can give the impression that the objects are floating. To solve this and other issues, you can use the **Shadow** effect found under the **World** tab.

The **Shadow correction** setting helps you to correct shadow offset from the object, but there are other settings that are worth keeping in mind:

- **Sun shadow range** can be used to tweak shadows' quality, but higher values will make objects far away lose their shadows

- **Ambient scale**, **Ambient**, and **Ambient diffuse** need to be perfectly balanced to remove some blotchiness that may appear in corners and other areas where two surfaces are very close to each other

Realistic reflections with the Reflection effect

Even when using the reflection control ball, the glass reflections may not look that good for close-up images. For these situations, you have the **Reflection** effect found under the **World** tab, which provides realistic and accurate reflections.

 Lumion 5 allows a reflection plane to be added to a water plane or a water material.

The process to apply this effect is very simple and you may feel tempted to add reflection planes to every single surface in the scene. That is not wise for several reasons. Firstly, you can only have 10 reflection planes in each scene and secondly, each reflection plane will mirror the entire scene, which means that each new reflection plane will have a massive impact on your scene.

A good way of solving this issue is by making all the glazing on each facade a single mesh with low polygon count.

Two-point perspective effect

While tweaking and adjusting the camera, sometimes it is necessary for you to correct the camera's perspective and for that you can use the two-point perspective effect. But why is that necessary? Have a look at the following comparison between the camera with and without this effect:

Because Lumion uses a three-point perspective, sometimes the camera angle can make the objects look taller and stretched, as you can see from the previous screenshot in the left-hand image. However, sometimes we need to straighten the vertical lines in the scene irrespective of the camera angle. That is when the two-point perspective comes into play to correct the camera and make your scene more eye-pleasing without strange angles and distortions.

Improving illumination with Global Illumination and Hyperlight®

The exterior lighting is often very simple and you only need to worry about the sun's position to render different moods. However, things get a little bit trickier when working with interior scenes and in particular, when there are no windows or when they are small. Primarily, Lumion uses the sun to light the scene but only a few rays of light will hit the interior of your scene and, for that reason, one thing you should start doing is making good use of lights.

But that leads to another problem we have covered previously in this book: too many lights will produce shadows that in turn make the scene heavy and increase the render time. However, Lumion provides a fantastic effect called **Global Illumination** that you can find under the **World** tab. What is the best way to use this effect in Lumion?

This effect substantially improves the interior lighting by simulating global illumination, which provides more realistic lighting. What is global illumination? In simple terms, it is a group of algorithms that help to produce more realistic lighting by taking into consideration not only the light that comes from light sources (sun, spotlights), but also the light reflected by objects and that is bouncing around the scene.

There are two ways you can use this effect:

- The first one involves scenes that are lit only by exterior light, like the sun. For that reason, you need to use the **Sun amount** settings to tweak how much the sun influences the interior lighting, the **Falloff speed** settings to tweak the smoothness of the interior light, and the **Reduce spots** settings in case you have some artifacts with extreme values. It is always a good idea to use a fill light as a helper to produce a nice interior lighting, even if you want to only use the sun as your main source.

- The second way you can use this effect is when working with interior lighting, like spotlights and fill lights. Creating a light rig for an interior scene involves a balanced use of Lumion's lights and the Global Illumination effect. You may feel tempted to fill the room with loads of lights but that is not going to help you. The first step is adding one single light to the scene and adding the Global Illumination effect, as shown in the following screenshot:

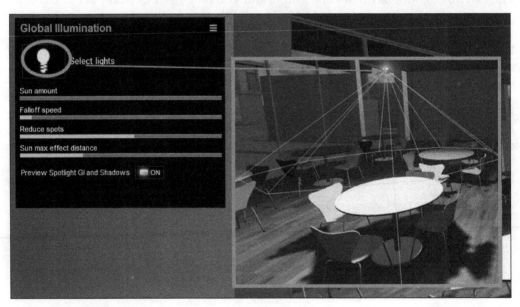

- The next step is for you to use the **Spotlight GI amount** slider (at the bottom) to start to increase the effect of that light into the scene. Eventually, you will realize that even a single light drastically improves the interior lighting quality. Even if you have multiple lights, try this effect with just two or three because the render time will not increase too much.

Maybe you find the Global Illumination too difficult to set up or perhaps discover the render time increased because of this effect. In that case, you may want to use **Hyperlight®**. Hyperlight® is a proprietary technology developed specifically for Lumion 5 and this technology is a physically-based method of incorporating light reflections into a scene, improving the light quality. Where can you find this Hyperlight® feature? Have a look at the following screenshot:

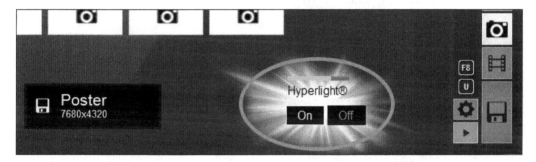

As you can see, this option can be either **On** or **Off** and then you tweak the intensity of the effect using the slider. A downside of this feature is that there is no preview to see how Hyperlight® is affecting the scene. You need to actually render a preview and adjust accordingly.

Another aspect you will certainly notice is that this effect will increase the noise present in the render but there is a way you can tackle this issue. Render a bigger image and then resize the image in Photoshop or GIMP; this will help to reduce some of the noise.

Summary

No doubt you are now well-equipped to create stunning still images with Lumion. You started with a quick introduction to **Photo** mode to recall some useful features and then you learned a wide variety of effects that are essential to create beautiful renders. Shadows, reflections, camera corrections, and good quality lighting are all small details that when assembled together have a dramatic effect on the final output you can achieve with Lumion.

Now that you know how to create still images, in the next chapter you will learn the best techniques to create clips that in turn can transform into amazing animations. You'll learn how composition is a powerful tool to create interesting clips and how to use Lumion's effects to mimic real-world camera features.

8
Producing a Movie with Lumion

Moving forward with the Lumion workflow, we are getting to one of the strongest features in Lumion: the possibility of effortlessly creating an animation and then exporting a video. However, the fact that it is easy to create an animation doesn't mean that Lumion is going to do all the hard work for you. The artistic decision of how you frame the subject and create a compelling composition is entirely your job. To help you with this perhaps daunting task, this chapter is going to cover some features and techniques essential for a successful video. The following list shows what we will be discussing in this chapter:

- Quick overview–**Movie** mode
- Creating efficient camera paths
- Working with clips
- Composition–a useful tool
- Adding realism with effects
- Depth of field and vignette effects for extra realism
- Using the **Motion blur** effect
- Adding sound effects
- Create a presentation with **Titles**

These topics are only the tip of the iceberg in particular when referring to how to use composition as a tool. This means that it is only through practice and experience that you will manage to grasp all the techniques and start to understand when and how to use them. But for now, let's start with some useful features in Lumion to create movies.

A quick overview – the Movie mode

The **Movie** mode allows you three options to create a movie. Two of these options involve importing an image or a video file to create a clip and, in addition, it is possible to apply most of Lumion's available effects to the imported files. These two options are very useful because they eliminate the need for an external movie editor to add an image or another video the client may require. The third option is when you use the **Record** button to create an animation using the scene you built in Lumion. However, there is more involved than just using the **Take Photo** button to create the camera path.

Creating efficient camera paths

In Lumion, you create a clip by using camera paths. This process involves defining the initial and end camera position, and Lumion filling the gap between each photo you take.

 For some camera paths where you need accurate control over the camera position, don't forget to use *Spacebar + WSAD* and *QE* to get a slow camera speed.

Eventually, you'll start to introduce more camera positions in the camera path and, in some situations, this can cause issues. The problem starts when you drastically change the camera orientation and the animation ends up with odd movements. This happens when you create something like this:

This is a classic example of pushing Lumion's limits because there is a dramatic change of orientation from the first camera position to the second one. In a situation like this, Lumion tries to create a smooth path between the two positions but the end result shows each adjustment that Lumion makes between the two camera angles. The solution for this is easy, as you can see in the following screenshot:

By adding a few more camera positions, there is a smooth transition between each camera and Lumion has more information to come up with a smoother camera path. You probably noticed that the distance between each camera position is very similar, if not equal. This is very important if you want to keep the same speed throughout the clip.

If, for example, two cameras are too close to each other and a third camera is far away, the end result will have a very slow start, then suddenly Lumion will speed up for the third and final position. To have consistency throughout the animation, you need to have an equal distance between cameras.

Working with clips

Clips are essential to create a movie and the way you control these clips can make a big difference. Things like copying, deleting, and moving clips are not difficult tasks, so we are going to cover some tips to increase productivity. When recording a clip, notice the buttons next to the viewport, as shown in the screenshot:

They may not look that significant but these buttons do wonders, and instead of using trial and error to get correct values, these tools provide a quick and effective way to do so. The **Camera Up and Down** button is useful when you need to keep the same camera height throughout the clip, increasing the accuracy of your shots.

Another useful feature that creates believable movies is the **Set eye level at 1.60** button, which sets the camera height to the standard 1.60 meters of height. This is the normal height from which a person gets his or her perspective and would be able to see the environment and in the building.

The **Horizontal eye level** feature is not something new because you could have access to this using the *Ctrl + H* key combination, but it is still nice to have everything in one place which saves you time and helps you to keep focused when creating or adjusting a camera path.

Composition–a useful tool

Before we even start with this section, there is something you need to understand: this book is not about composition, and the goal of this section is not to detail step-by-step how to create good compositions.

So what is the point? The main goal is to make you aware that creating good movies in Lumion is not a simple fact of pointing the camera at something and starting to record. To create a successful animation, it is essential that you at least have a good understanding of these guidelines:

- **Rule of thirds**: This is basically a compositional guideline and it states that when you divide, vertically or horizontally, the screen in three equal sections, these virtual lines show points of interest that help to create tension and an interesting composition. These points are called focal points because our eyes are naturally drawn to them and for that reason we can place interesting aspects of our scene there. You may notice when adjusting the camera in the **Movie** or **Photo** mode, there is a thin grid that appears to help you to see where these points are.

- **Depth of field** and **Leading lines**: The goal of these techniques is to lead the viewer's eye where you want to. Depth of field (DOF), in particular, can create a very dynamic clip if you animate the focus going from one point to another. You can use straight, diagonal, and curved lines to create depth and a sense of movement.

- **Foreground/Background**: When shooting an image or movie, the camera's lens can sometimes flatten the foreground and background, and this removes most of the depth. A good way to ensure you add depth to an image or shot is by using different elements in the foreground, middle ground, and background. This works because our eye recognizes these layers of information and this in turn creates a more interesting composition.

- **Framing**: This involves using foreground and middle ground objects to work as frames for your subject. For example, a classic example is using trees to naturally create a frame for the subject.

To help you learn more about some of these techniques, have a look at the following website:

`http://compositionstudy.com/`

The best way to learn is by studying how the masters use these techniques to produce stunning photos.

As you can see, this is only a tiny parcel of techniques available and how they can be used. Keep in mind that the goal of composition is to guide the viewer's attention to the main subject of what you are showing. A video with a lack of composition will confuse the viewer since he or she will not be able to really understand where to focus his or her attention.

A great example of camera shots can be found in the movie, *The Third and Seventh*, by Alex Roman. It is a masterpiece in all senses and provides good examples to study and apply to your work.

Another step to producing believable renders and, in this case, movies is the appropriate use of Lumion's effects.

Adding realism with Lumion's effects

Using effects is not something new because you have been using them all along in this book. The previous chapter covered some effects that can also be used in the **Movie** mode, such as sun study, shadow, reflection, two-point perspective, and Global Illumination. All of these effects can be used for a movie and you only need to be careful with the two-point perspective which may not work well with an extreme camera angle. However, what other effects can you use to add realism to the animation?

The depth of field and Vignette effects

The next two effects are related to photo-realism because both of them happen when you use a real camera. In simple words, **depth of field** in a photograph is the distance between the nearest and farthest objects that are in focus and acceptably sharp. Why should you care about this?

Depth of field is a tool that can help to guide the viewers' attention to the areas you want without any distractions. It can also be used to separate objects from the background making them stand out and, when used correctly, depth of field can have a deep impact both on the art and quality of the photograph.

Being an aide for creating believable renders, it's no surprise that an effect called depth of field is available. This is not the easiest effect to use in Lumion and for that reason, here is some explanation on what each setting does:

- **Focus distance**: This specifies where the camera should focus. If you start with a value of 1, you can see on the bottom section a strip of clear sharpness, then you can increase the value until that section reaches the area that you want to be in focus.

- **F stop**: With this setting, keep in mind that higher values remove the blur and lower values can be used to create a bokeh effect.

- **Smoothness**: This is used to create sharper edges, but you probably should leave this at 1.

- **Isolate foreground**: This controls the depth of field layers in front of the camera but usually doesn't produce a good result.

- **Expansion**: This works great for close-ups to get a sharper look at the 3D model in focus.

The following screenshot can help you understand the benefits of using depth of field and other effects that mimic a real camera:

It may be difficult to perceive all the effects and, in particular, depth of field but certainly there is a big difference between the two images. The image on the right-hand side shows a few more effects that can be used to increase the image quality and one of them is the **Vignette**. Essentially, a vignette is a natural gradual darkening that happens in almost every camera, in particular when using a wide-angle lens. But a vignette can be used as a composition tool as well, helping the viewer to focus his or her attention to a specific point on the image. In Lumion, this effect can be found under the **Artistic** tab, but keep in mind that the vignette needs to be of something subtle in order to work.

There are a few more effects you may want to have a look at, such as **Noise** and **Chromatic aberrations**. These effects can help a lot to make the image look more natural and this is because both of them are a natural result of using a real camera, but again don't overuse it. All these effects need to be applied in a very subtle way; otherwise, the viewer will get distracted with a ridiculous vignette or chromatic aberration. There is another effect that is essential in any animation you create.

The motion blur effect

To take a photograph, you need to expose the film or the sensor of the camera to light. When shooting a movie, there will always be some amount of motion blur caused by objects that are moving and because of the exposure settings. Although in most situations, this motion blur is very subtle and it is essential that we add motion blur to the movie; otherwise our brain notices there is something missing.

This is one of the easiest effects to add because unless you want something very extreme, the default values will be enough for the animation. A good practice is adding this effect not to each clip individually but instead to the entire movie.

This effect is extremely clever because the amount of motion blur is proportional to the camera speed. So, if the camera is static or there aren't any moving objects, the amount of blur will be close to none and this avoids the effect having to be animated. This is shown in the following screenshot:

On the left-hand side the camera is moving and, for that reason, the **Motion blur** effect does a good job of adding a realistic motion blur effect to the video. On the other hand, with regard to the image on the right hand side, the camera is not moving at all and for that reason no motion blur is visible, which makes sense since this effect only occurs with moving objects or cameras.

Extra detail with sound effects

Sound is almost essential in any movie you create; even the silent movies had someone playing a piano. Sound brings life to the movie and can play with viewers' emotions. In line with this, Lumion provides the opportunity to add sounds to the scene that are played while moving around. The process to add and tweak these sounds is very simple, as shown in the following screenshot:

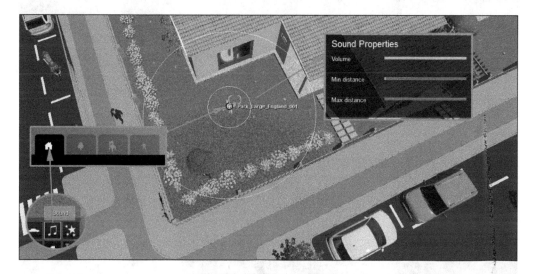

After placing the sound, you can use the **Sound Properties** effect to tweak the areas that this sound affects. But sometimes the **Max distance** value may be too big for your scene. A good way to solve this is by scaling down the sound like you would do to another object.

Back in **Movie** mode, you can import an audio file (WAV format only) using the **Sound** effect. However, you can only find this effect under the **Objects** tab if the **Entire Movie** button is pressed.

Creating a presentation with Titles

If your main goal for the animation is to provide a project presentation, you may want to have a look at the **Titles** effect. This effect lets you add text to the movie and create professional presentations. The main options of this effect are shown in the following screenshot:

You need to press the **Titles** button in order to access these options:

- Adding a logo to the presentation (refer to image **1**)
- Choosing the text's style presented on the screen (refer to image **2**)
- Choosing the text's location on the screen (refer to image **3**)
- You can select one of the twelve text fonts available, or press the **Custom** button to select another font installed on your system (refer to image **4**)
- Select the text's color that is presented (refer to image **5**)

However, instead of doing this for every single clip in the movie, don't forget to use the copy and paste functions available in each effect.

Summary

As a continuation of the last chapter, you have now learned some of the best practices to produce and create a movie. In the first sections, you learned how to efficiently build smoother camera paths. Adding to this knowledge, you also learned the importance of using composition while creating the clips, and some explanations of common composition rules.

Again, there is much more that could be said on this subject but with practice and experience, you will learn how to use composition in an efficient way. Then, you learned how to enhance the quality of the final image by using Lumion's effects that allow real camera features to create a believable movie. Finally, you saw how to use sounds to bring your scene to life and how to use the **Titles** effect to create presentations.

The next and final chapter covers how to export the animation (and still images), and some final thoughts on how to use post production to create a final piece of a beautiful artwork.

9
Exporting and Post Production

Welcome to the final stage of the process to create a stunning Lumion architectural visualization. The final step is exporting the 3D scene built in Lumion to a format that can be easily shared with the whole world. As seen in the previous two chapters, there are two ways you can present your work: by using a still image or by creating an animation.

However, how can you export these formats? What is the best way to do it? And can you enhance the look of the final output? To help you with these final steps, this chapter was prepared to tackle some of the best techniques and the following list gives you a fair idea of what we will be covering:

- Optimizing before rendering
- Different file format options
- Using the **Movie** mode to produce still images
- Rendering with the **Movie** mode
- Exporting movies versus clips
- Rendering an image sequence
- What are render passes
- How to use render passes–SkyAlpha, Material ID, SpecularReflection, and Depthmap
- Using the Lumion viewer

Where do we start? Well, let's start by taking a good look at how you can decrease the render time, in particular when exporting movies.

Optimizing before rendering

Now that you know how to render a movie and a still image, it is time to export your scene. Exporting a still image may take a couple seconds but when working with movies you may start to worry and in some situations, panic. The reason for this is because you don't have one still image to render; you have 15000 frames (a 10 minute movie with 25fps), and if each frame takes 1 minute to render that means you need 250 hours to render 10 minutes.

First of all, keep in mind that the graphics card makes all the difference, and there is nothing in this world that will make the render go faster. However, you can help by making smart choices. Let's start with the first:

- **Global Illumination effect**: This effect takes a toll on the render time. Personally, I have seen render times cut by half when this effect is removed. The solution for not using this effect is a good use of the fill light and you will probably need a couple of these lights with a low intensity in your scene.

- **Lights**: Do you really need your lights to have the **Accuracy** option selected? Do you think you could use **Speed** instead? Changing this simple option can make a big impact on the time render, in particular if you have several lights present.

- **Reflection effect**: This is perhaps the second primary effect that makes the scene really, really slow. Each reflection plane mirrors the entire scene and if you have more than one maybe you should consider using the reflection control ball.

- **Shadow and Clouds quality**: Starting with the Shadow effect, see if the **HQ Soft Shadow** makes a big difference in the final quality, and perhaps you will have to reduce the **Final Render Sun Shadow Detail** from **Super** to **High** or even to **Normal**. Regarding the **Clouds** effect, you may want to turn off the **HQ clouds in movie render** option.

And some final advice, always restart Lumion before rendering a movie. Next, we will see what is available to export the scene you have built in Lumion.

The different file formats to export from Lumion

Starting with the **Photo** mode, technically you are constrained to four sizes, as shown in the following screenshot:

What if you need a different image size? The only option is to render a bigger image and then resize it.

 Resizing the image will also contribute to creating a sharper image.

The only downside is that if you want to do some color correction and other adjustments, you only can export an 8 bit image (which doesn't give you much room for tweaking colors) and use these formats:

- **Joint Photographic Experts Group**: *.jpg
- **Bitmap**: *.bmp
- **DirectDraw Surface**: *.dds
- **Portable Network Graphics**: *.png
- **Truevision Graphics Adapter**: *.tga

As mentioned before, this is one option to export a still image and although the **Photo** mode provides a friendly interface, there is a better option that makes all the processes easier.

Using the Movie mode to export still images

The question is: is it possible for you to use the **Movie** mode to export still images? Not only can you do this but also the entire workflow is even better because instead of having to export one image at time, it is possible to export as many images as you want. Still, the question is: how?

Let's start by opening the **Movie** mode and for this exercise, creating a clip with 4 photos (or more if you want to). When you take photos the goal here is not to create a camera path. Instead, see each photo as the camera viewpoint you want to export as a still image. Then, select the **Save Movie** button and the following options appear:

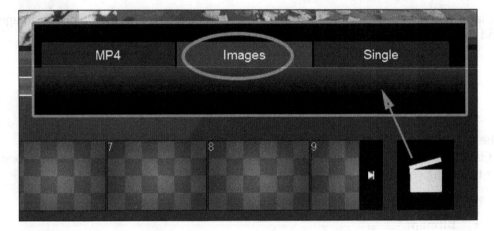

You need to select the **Images** tab and then you are presented with several options to export images, as shown in the following screenshot:

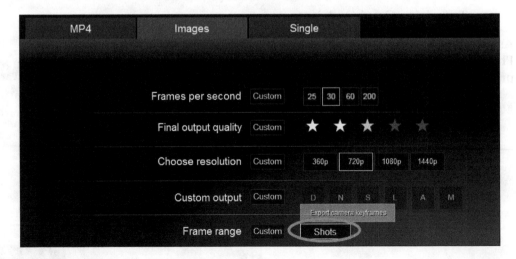

In this instance, you only need to worry about the **Final output quality** and the **Choose resolution** options. Now, pay attention to the **Frame range** option and if, in your case, it says **Auto** click on the button until it appears as the option shown in the preceding screenshot–**Shots**.

 One downside of this option is that the biggest image you can save is only 2560x1440 pixels. In the **Photo** mode, the biggest image size is 7680x4320 pixels.

If you noticed from the previous screenshot above, the **Shots** option says that this option exports the camera keyframes or, in other words, it is only going to export the photos you used to create the camera path. So, if you only used four photos, it is only going to export four photos. This is one of the best practices when exporting still images because if the project has several still images, it can be tedious and time-consuming exporting every individual image. This is like doing a batch render.

One word of caution: if you use the option **Create movie from clip**, the photos exported are only the ones used for that particular clip but if you use the main button called **Save Movie**, the photos exported are from all the clips in the movie.

Rendering using the Movie mode

Before we go even further, there is another good practice you should take into consideration. The reality is that you can watch a movie over and over on the viewport but it is only when you export a movie that you can perceive some errors and mistakes. For that reason, it is time-saving exporting a movie with draft quality but with a relatively good resolution. Initially, this may sound counter-productive, but it helps you in checking if there is a need for any further adjustment at the same time, it is something you can send to the client to receive the final approval.

We covered still images but what about exporting a movie? The first decision you need to make is how you are going to export the movie, and the following screenshot shows the two possibilities you have in doing so:

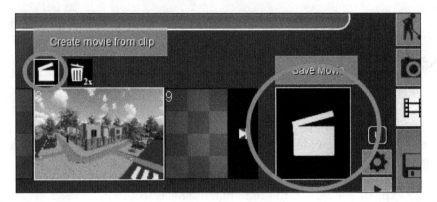

The **Save Movie** button assembles all the clips into a big movie and this may be something you want when working with small animations. However, when you have a movie around 5 minutes long, using the **Create a movie from a clip** option is a better solution. Why? It gives you flexibility and more control over the movie.

If you export an entire movie and Lumion crashes, you have to start all over again. If you export an entire movie and there is something wrong that needs to be corrected, you know what is going to happen? Yes, you will have to render the whole movie again. And we could carry on with even more problems that really happen in a production environment that force you to render the entire movie again, which is time-consuming and not practical at all.

So, saving individual clips may not be that practical because you have to export it one by one, but it allows you a safety net that can save time and resources. Why? Because if something is wrong, you just need to render one clip again and not the entire movie. Now that you have decided how to export the movie, the next question is: how?

Rendering an image sequence

When clicking on the **Save Movie** button, the initial option available is the **MP4** tab and the options to export are very simple: select the FPS desired, then the quality, and finally the image size and after a couple hours you have the mp4 file ready to go.

Although there is nothing wrong with this option, you can export a sequence of images instead of an mp4 file. An mp4 file is only useful if you are planning to do some post production using the render passes available. When exporting the clip or the movie, the tab you want to use is the **Images** tab that you used before to export a set of images. Do you still remember the **Frame range** setting with the **Shots** option? If you press again on that button a new option appears, as shown in the following screenshot:

The **Range** option lets you specify which frames you want to export and if you place the mouse over the two text boxes, a small preview appears of each frame, which is useful when rendering specific sections of the movie or clip.

After this, you only have to click on the **Start movie** export button to select a location and start rendering the movie. Keep in mind that you will be rendering 25 or 30 images for each second, and that means you need loads of space to save all those images. However, what is the point of all this work? As mentioned, we need to make some adjustments using the render passes.

What is a render pass?

As previously discussed, a benefit of exporting a range of frames is that you can later tweak Lumion's output and perform color correction and other adjustments. To make your life easier, Lumion allows you to export along with a range of frames some render passes, as shown in the following screenshot:

The **Custom output** is where you can find all the render passes available. Each letter corresponds to a render pass that is explained in the following list:

- **Depthmap (D)**: This is a grayscale map with information regarding the distance of the 3D models from the camera.

- **Normalmap (N)**: This is similar to the one used to create bumps in the materials, but this render pass doesn't have many useful applications.

- **SpecularReflection map (S)**: This render pass stores information regarding the surface highlights and reflections.

- **Lighting map (L)**: This render pass stores light and brightness information for each surface in the scene.

- **SkyAlpha map (A)**: This is a black-and-white image that works as a mask and can be used to replace the sky with a different one or control the sky without affecting the rest of the image.

- **Material ID (M)**: A color or ID is assigned to each material used in the scene. This render pass is used to isolate areas and tweak the colors in the image.

This information is great but how can you use it in a practical way? Well, before we move to a more complex subject you need to keep in mind that:

- Firstly, some of the techniques presented here are not the final word on this topic which means you are free to explore the use of render passes in other ways.

- Secondly, you better have a big hard drive to accommodate all the images generated by Lumion. If the animation is comprised of 3000 frames, multiply that by the number of render passes you selected to give you the final amount of images you will have. To give you an idea, if you have 3000 frames and if you use all six render passes you will end up with 18000 images.

Practical ways to use the render passes

Before we even start, the question that arises is: what do you need to work with render passes? If you are working with still images, an image editor like Photoshop or GIMP is more than enough to handle this task. But when working with all those frames, you need a way to transform and convert them into a video.

A good solution is using the amazingly powerful Fusion7 developed by Blackmagic Design. This is a very robust and professional application that is free to use.

> Blackmagic design provides two versions. The free version is called Fusion 7. The paid version is called Fusion 7 Studio and contains a few more features that are not that necessary for this kind of work.
>
> You can find more information here:
>
> https://www.blackmagicdesign.com

However, we will try to keep these next sections software agnostic in order to suit everyone. The concept is explained here and certainly by knowing the tools provided you can easily achieve the same result.

Using the SkyAlpha render pass

The SkyAlpha render pass only has two colors (black and white) and you can use these colors to create masks that are extremely useful in adjusting specific areas in the image, as shown in the following screenshot:

In this situation, the SkyAlpha render pass was used to replace Lumion's sky with another one. But the use of this render pass doesn't stop here because you can use it to adjust the vegetation without affecting the sky. And if you want to go even further, you can hide all the geometry except for the plants, render a frame with the SkyAlpha as custom output, and then you will have a proper mask to work on and adjust all the plants in the scene. Nevertheless, you may be asking: is that not the purpose of the Material ID render pass?

Material ID – do's and don'ts

The Material ID render pass assigns a color to each 3D model present in the scene and this is extremely useful to again tweak certain areas of the image without affecting the whole image. Have a look at the following screenshot to see how you can use this render pass:

For this example, the roof's color was changed to a very bright red to exemplify how easy it is to isolate certain areas and tweak them without affecting the rest of the image.

Although you'll want to use this technique to work and adjust areas in the image, you definitely should not use this render pass to tweak any plants present in the scene. If you look closely at the trees in the Material ID render pass, notice that instead of a well-defined leaf you have a plane, and this makes the Material ID useless in tweaking any vegetation. Instead, you need to use the SkyAlpha technique mentioned in the previous section.

Adjusting reflections and lighting

The next render pass that can be used to drastically improve the image's look is the SpecularReflection and Lighting render passes. Both of these render passes can only be used with the aid of blending modes that are available in most image editors. There isn't any secret formula to working with these render passes because **Soft light blending** mode may work for one image but, for others, you might find that **Screen blending** mode does a better job.

However, you need to use both of these render passes in small amounts and don't forget that the main goal is to correct areas that don't look that good, not to redo an entire image. In other words, if you are happy with the reflections, don't change them. The last render pass that is extremely useful is the depthmap render pass.

Faking depth of field

The depthmap render pass is a time-saver. Using the depth of field effect sometimes can be a challenge to get right and it also increases the render time. With the depthmap render pass, you can add depth of field in the post production process, which in turn provides you more flexibility over the final result. How can you do that? This is something that depends on the application you are using and you must understand that we simply cannot cover every single application.

For example, in Photoshop there is a filter called **Lens Blur** that can use this depthmap render pass to create a realistic depth of field. But the key point of this topic is that you can fake depth of field with this render pass, and it is worth exploring how you can do this with your favorite application.

 While exploring how to create depth of field, please keep in mind that in some applications, the depthmap is also called Z-depth map.

But the use for the depthmap doesn't end here because in addition, you can add haze or fog to the render. This technique again saves you the hassle of using Lumion's fog to achieve the same effect and adds some realism to the render. How can you do that? This technique is easier to explain because the majority of the image editor has blending modes for the layers.

The simplest way to use it is by inverting the depthmap and then using the **Soft light blending** mode to create the haze effect. Don't forget that you need to always adjust the opacity or intensity of these effects and even sometimes use a mask to hide the effect in certain areas. If you are using Photoshop, there is an additional technique in which you may be interested.

To create a blend between layers, Photoshop has an option called **Blend** that can be found under the **Layer Style** window. This is an advanced method that blends one layer into another based on the content of either of the two layers. You can use this feature to tweak where the haze or fog starts and even create a nice transition. Have a closer look at the following screenshot:

In this instance, the depthmap render pass is placed over the normal image without the **Soft Light blending** mode applied so it can be easier to perceive what is happening. For this image, we didn't want the fog to start right in front of the camera because this haze or fog effect usually happens at a certain distance from the camera. It's true that you can tackle this issue by using a mask and hiding the effect in certain areas but by using **Blend** you can adjust where this effect starts.

Start by moving the handle that controls the black areas and see how the fog starts to move forward. However, the line is too harsh and not realistic at all and the reason is you need to break the handle, as shown in the following screenshot:

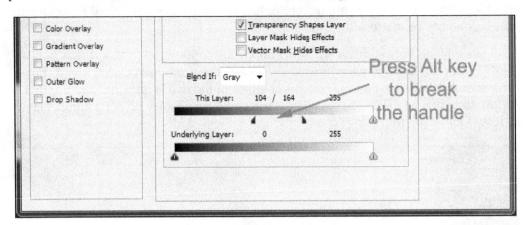

Press the *Alt* key and click on the handle to break it into sections. Now you can create a gradient between values, which in turns allow us to create a smooth transition, more pleasing to the eye.

A final word on this matter of doing some post production after rendering the movie or the still image: some of the effects that Lumion offers such as Vignette, Noise, Chromatic aberrations and other effects, can be done with external applications and in some situations will produce better results. Removing these effects will also help to decrease the render time and allow more flexibility on how they are applied.

Using Lumion Viewer to present a project

Lumion Viewer is one possibility for presenting a project. The advantage of using Lumion Viewer is that the client can walk around and explore the scene created.

Lumion Viewer is a separate application available for licensed Pro users. You can provide a Viewer installer for a client to install the base viewer application on their system. The client then double-clicks or uses **Open File** from the Viewer to open the project.

This all sounds really great but, on the other hand, the client needs to download and install a file of almost 6GB plus the scene. On top of this, the client needs to have a good graphic card otherwise the viewport will literally drag, begging for more resources.

However, this option may prove useful at meetings with the client where you can demonstrate the work in progress and receive valuable feedback.

Summary

In this chapter, you learned that there is more involved in the process of saving and exporting the scene you created in Lumion. One of the most important sections was no doubt on how to optimize your scene in order to reduce the render time. Then, you explored more of how to render the scene and also the flexibility you have by using the **Movie** mode to export a set of images. Regarding rendering a movie, you learned that there are good reasons to render clips instead of an entire movie and also that it is possible to render a sequence of images.

This only proves useful if you are planning to do some post production and you saw practical applications to use at least four render passes in order to enhance the final quality of your work.

What is the next step? You may want to explore in more depth what is available in Lumion, as well as other techniques that weren't covered here. Two books that are worth checking out are the *Lumion 3D Cookbook* and *Mastering Lumion 3D*.

The first book, *Lumion 3D Cookbook*, covers more than 100 recipes and works as a reference guide to using Lumion. Although some of the more recent features aren't covered (they were covered here), it is still useful since Lumion's interface and features are the same. If you want to quickly know how something is done in Lumion, *Lumion 3D Cookbook* is the book you'll need.

The second book provides a more in-depth approach where every single Lumion feature is covered and explained with practical steps. With *Mastering Lumion 3D*, you will not miss anything from Lumion. The most important chapters are, without a doubt, the ones that cover some filming and composition techniques that are essential to creating interesting and appealing visualizations. But it only gives you the basics to start working; after that, you have to practice, practice, and practice.

Index

Symbols

3D animations
exporting 21, 22
3Delicious
URL 7
3D models
adding 36
checking 36
controlling, filters used 29, 30
detailing 36
duplicating, with Alt key 44
edges, beveling 37
importing 16, 17
interior scenes, populating 41
multiple copies with random
    sizes, placing 26
placing 26
placing, Mass Placement tool used 27, 28
properties, editing 44, 45
refining 36
updating 32
3D models, importing
3D animations, exporting 21, 22
common problems 22-26
from 3ds Max, using COLLADA 18
from 3ds Max, using FBX 18
missing faces 24
reference link 18
reversed faces 24
rookie mistakes 22, 23
settings, exporting for COLLADA
    files 19, 20
settings, exporting for FBX files 18, 19
SketchUp files, importing 17
solutions 25, 26

A

Advanced move effect
curved paths 99, 100
animation
exporting, tips 94
imported animations, controlling 97
importing 96
scene, planning 94
with Move effect 97, 98
ArchiCAD
URL 6
Archive 3D
URL 7
Autodesk FBX format 18

B

Blackmagic design
about 133
URL 133
Blender
URL 5

C

camera
controlling 12, 13
camera paths
creating 114, 115
clips
creating 116
Clouds effect 126
coast
creating, Ocean menu used 61
creating, Terrain menu used 61

COLLADA
settings, exporting 19, 20
used, for importing 3D models from 3ds
Max 18
composition
about 116, 117
depth of field (DOF) 117
Foreground/Background 117
framing 117
leading lines 117
rule of thirds 117
URL 117
Creative Crash
URL 7

D

depth of field (DOF)
faking 136-138
settings 118
using 118, 119

E

effects library 39
elements
scattering, Grass menu used 68, 69
Emissive setting 80-82
Evermotion
URL 7
Export scene 56-59

F

FBX
settings, exporting 18, 19
used, for importing 3D models from 3ds
Max 18
file formats
about 127
for exporting 127
Movie mode, using 128, 129
fill light
placing 51, 52
versus, omni light and spotlight 52, 53
filters
used, for controlling 3D models 29, 30

frames per second (FPS) 9

G

GIMP DDS plugin
URL 65
Global Data Explorer
URL 66
Global Illumination
about 109, 126
used, for improving illumination 109-111
glossiness 49
glossiness map
creating 91, 92
glowing materials 80-82
Grass menu
used, for scattering elements 68, 69

H

heightmaps
creating, guidelines for 64, 65
creating, tools used 65-67
used, for creating terrain 64
Height menu
used, for creating valley 62, 63
highlights
fixing, on textures 88
Hyperlight®
about 111
used, for improving illumination 109-111

I

image sequence
rendering 131
Import scene 56-59
indoor library 39
interface
exploring 12, 13
interior scenes, populating with 3D models
3D model properties, editing 44, 45
Alt key, using 44
Context menu, using 42, 43
Replace with library selection option 46
rotate option, using 43, 44
Select in library option, using 46, 47

L

Landsat TM
  URL 66
landscape
  coast creating, Ocean menu used 61
  coast creating, Terrain menu used 61
  creating, with Landscape menu 59, 60
  heightmaps creation, guidelines 64
  heightmaps, creating with tools 65-67
  selecting, Paint menu used 69, 70
  terrain creating, heightmaps used 64
  types 61
  valley creating, Height menu used 62, 63
  valley creating, Water menu used 62, 63
Large 3D Terrain (L3DT)
  URL 66
large scenes
  handling 30-32
  importing 30-32
LatLong
  URL 107
layers
  using 8-10
lights
  about 126
  adding 51
  adjusting 136
  fill light, placing 51, 52
  omni light, placing 51
  shadows, adding 53, 54
  spotlight, placing 51, 52
lights and utilities library 40
Lumion
  about 11
  additional models, using 7
  advantages 2, 3
  animation, techniques 93
  camera, controlling 12, 13
  disadvantages 4
  for beginners 2
  hardware, URL 5
  interface, exploring 12, 13
  layers, using 8, 9
  materials 74
  project, organizing 7, 8
  requisites 5
  URL 2
  versions 6
Lumion 3D
  limitations 1
Lumion Pro
  effects library 39
  indoor library 39
  lights and utilities library 40
  nature library 38
  outdoor library 39
  people and animals library 39
  sound library 38
  transport library 38
Lumion Viewer
  using 138

M

Mass move effect
  using 100
Mass Placement tool
  used, for placing 3D models 27, 28
Material ID render pass
  using 135
materials
  about 10, 11, 72, 73
  creating, external 3D application used 86
  custom materials 85
  Emissive setting 81, 82
  glowing materials 80-82
  in Lumion 74
  normal map, tips for creating 76, 77
  normal map, using 75
  reflections, improving 82-84
  Standard material 87, 88
  using 74
  video, using as textures 84
Merge scene 56-59
missing faces 24
motion blur effect
  using 120
Move effect 98
Movie mode
  about 95, 96, 114
  camera paths, creating 114, 115
  clips, creating 116
  image sequence, rendering 131

rendering
    optimization, considerations 126
    with Movie mode 129, 130
render pass
    about 132
    Depthmap (D) 132
    depth of field, faking 136-138
    lighting, adjusting 136
    Lighting map (L) 132
    Material ID (M) 132, 135
    Normalmap (N) 132
    reflections, adjusting 136
    Sky alpha map (A) 132, 134
    SpecularReflection map (S) 132
    using 133
Resources Blogscopia
    URL 7
reversed faces 24
Revit
    URL 6

S

scene
    Export scene 56-59
    Import scene 56-59
    Merge scene 56-59
    planning 56
seamless textures
    creating 90
Shadow effect
    about 126
    used, for correcting shadows 107
shadows
    adding 53, 54
Simplygon
    URL 7
SketchUp
    URL 5
SketchUp files
    importing 17
SketchUp Warehouse
    URL 7
SkyAlpha render pass
    using 134
sound effects
    used, for extra detail 121

sound library 38
spotlight
    placing 51, 52
    versus, fill light and omni light 52, 53
Standard material
    about 87
    highlights, eliminating 88
    texture highlights, fixing 88, 89
    textures, finding 88
still images
    exporting, with Movie mode 128, 129
storyboard 94, 95
Sun Study
    using 107

T

Terragen
    about 66
    URL 66
terrain
    creating, heightmaps used 64
    imported terrains 68
    tools, working with 60
Terrain menu
    used, for creating coast 61
textures
    highlights, fixing 88
    video, using as 84
Titles
    presentation, creating 122
transport library 38
TurboSquid
    URL 7
two-point perspective effect
    using 108

U

US Geological Survey (USGS)
    about 66
    URL 66

V

valley
    creating, Height menu used 62, 63
    creating, Water menu used 62, 63

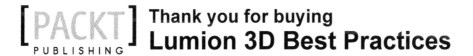

About Packt Publishing

Packt, pronounced 'packed', published its first book, *Mastering phpMyAdmin for Effective MySQL Management*, in April 2004, and subsequently continued to specialize in publishing highly focused books on specific technologies and solutions.

Our books and publications share the experiences of your fellow IT professionals in adapting and customizing today's systems, applications, and frameworks. Our solution-based books give you the knowledge and power to customize the software and technologies you're using to get the job done. Packt books are more specific and less general than the IT books you have seen in the past. Our unique business model allows us to bring you more focused information, giving you more of what you need to know, and less of what you don't.

Packt is a modern yet unique publishing company that focuses on producing quality, cutting-edge books for communities of developers, administrators, and newbies alike. For more information, please visit our website at www.packtpub.com.

Writing for Packt

We welcome all inquiries from people who are interested in authoring. Book proposals should be sent to author@packtpub.com. If your book idea is still at an early stage and you would like to discuss it first before writing a formal book proposal, then please contact us; one of our commissioning editors will get in touch with you.

We're not just looking for published authors; if you have strong technical skills but no writing experience, our experienced editors can help you develop a writing career, or simply get some additional reward for your expertise.

[PACKT]
PUBLISHING

Mastering Lumion 3D

ISBN: 978-1-78355-203-0   Paperback: 286 pages

Master the art of creating real-time 3D architectural visualizations using Lumion 3D

1. Create professional architectural visualizations in seconds using real-time technology.

2. Learn the inbuilt Lumion effects to enhance your project to an expert level.

3. Covers in-depth practical and real examples along with clear instructions to create real-time visualizations.

Lumion 3D Cookbook

ISBN: 978-1-78355-093-7   Paperback: 258 pages

Revolutionize your Lumion skills with over 100 recipes to create stunning architectural visualizations

1. Build spectacular architectural perceptions in seconds using real-time technology.

2. Learn how to apply the inbuilt effects in Lumion to enhance your project to a whole new level.

3. Bursting with practical examples, and simple, clear instructions to help you produce advanced visualizations with an expert level.

Getting Started with Lumion 3D

ISBN: 978-1-84969-949-5   Paperback: 134 pages

Create a professional architectural visualization in minutes using Lumion 3D

1. A beginner's guide to architectural visualization.

2. Tips and tricks for modelling, texturing, and rendering using Lumion 3D.

3. Add a special touch to your images with Photoshop.

Blender Cycles: Materials and Textures Cookbook
Third Edition

ISBN: 978-1-78439-993-1   Paperback: 400 pages

Over 40 practical recipes to create stunning materials and textures using the Cycles rendering engine with Blender

1. Create realistic material shaders by understanding the fundamentals of material creation in Cycles.

2. Quickly make impressive projects production-ready using the Blender rendering engine.

3. Discover step-by-step material recipes with complete diagrams of nodes.

Please check **www.PacktPub.com** for information on our titles

www.ingramcontent.com/pod-product-compliance
Lightning Source LLC
Chambersburg PA
CBHW060141060326
40690CB00018B/3935